# SWITCHBACK

The author with Sam on the top of Moose Peak in the Blackfeet National Forest in 1928.

# SWITCHBACK

*Fifty Years in Glacier & the West*

## W.J. YENNE

*Foreword by George Ostrom*

THE
History
PRESS

*Bill Yenne is an unusual breed of cowboy. He has the curiosity to probe, the intelligence to remember and the exceptional ability to consummate. The experiences and scenes that Charlie Russell could render on canvas Bill Yenne can interpret with words.*

—Phillip R. Iversen, Superintendent (Retired), Glacier National Park

*It's not easy to sit down and write about Bill Yenne. When I knew him he had a "soft government job"—as the Trail Supervisor at Glacier National Park. Glacier Park has a million spectacular mountain acres and over 1,000 miles of hiker and horse trails. All he really had to do was wrangle the men and money for 1,000 miles of maintenance, know all the trails and keep them all passable and safe. Bill brought his attributes of competence, knowledge, enthusiasm and humor to bear on as hard and diverse a job as anyone had in any park.*

—James W. Corson, Chief of Interpretation and Visitor Services (Retired), North Atlantic Region, National Park Service

*Bill Yenne, a friend of mine, has been familiar with professional rodeo since the days of the "Turtles," the early years of the Professional Rodeo Cowboys Association. He is both a charter and lifetime member of our Rodeo Historical Society and the Rodeo Hall of Fame "Wild Bunch."*

—Willard H. Porter, Director, Rodeo Division, National Cowboy Hall of Fame

Switchback *may not be quite as laced with colorful side notes as when Yenne gets wound up around a campfire, but it does capture the feeling he tried to impart to readers about the life he'd had. This book tells of the rugged trail life from the heart of one who lived and loved it.*

—National Park Service Courier

*If you've ever pulled a diamond hitch tight on a pack animal, or even thought about doing it, here's a book you'll enjoy. It's all about Bill Yenne's years of packing with mules and horses. There's a rodeo yarn or two, experiences with bronc mules and horses, and encounters with grizzly bears, too.*

—Western Horseman Magazine

Published by The History Press
Charleston, SC
www.historypress.com

This edition first published in 2019.

Manufactured in the United States

ISBN 9781467142731

Library of Congress Control Number: 2019935343

*Notice*: The information in this book is true and complete to the best of our knowledge. It is offered without guarantee on the part of the author or The History Press. The author and The History Press disclaim all liability in connection with the use of this book.

W.J. Yenne at Josephine Lake, with Grinnell Glacier in the background.

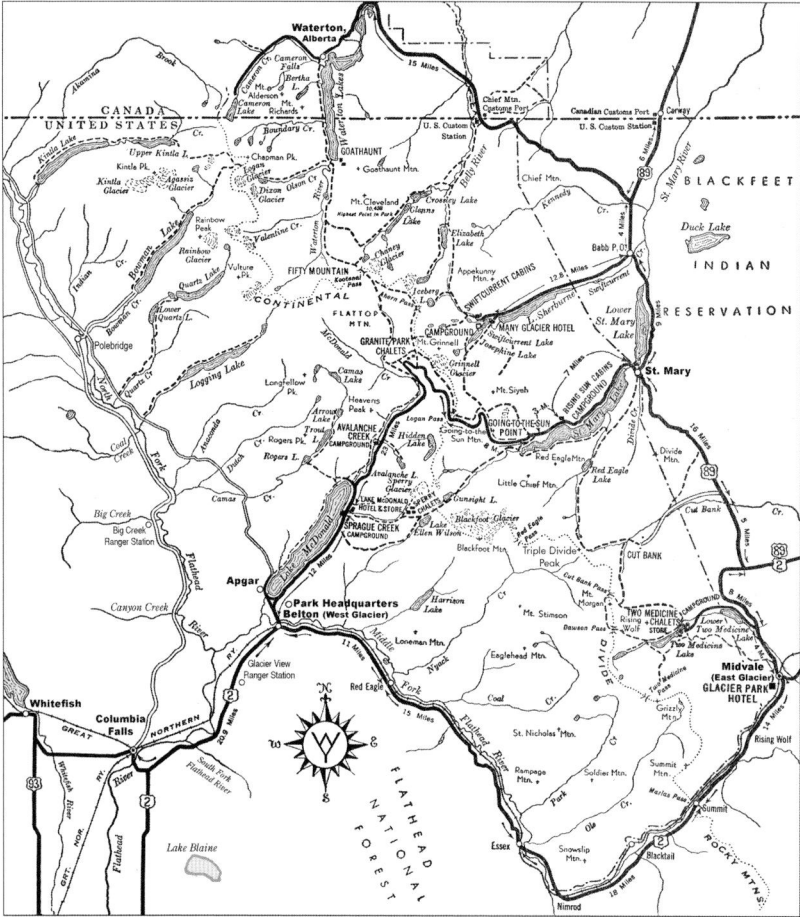

Glacier National Park, created in 1910, encompasses 1.013 million acres. Its western boundary is defined by the North Fork of the Flathead River and its southern boundary by the Middle Fork of the Flathead. Its eastern boundary is seen here as a dashed line, and its northern boundary is the international border with Canada. In 1932, it and Canada's Waterton Lakes National Park were designated as the Waterton-Glacier International Peace Park.

# CONTENTS

Foreword, by George Ostrom ................................................. 11

Introduction, by William P. Yenne ...................................... 15

1. Early Days in the Upper Flathead Lake Country .......... 19
2. Packing and Trail Building on the North Fork of
      the Flathead River .................................................. 27
3. The Year 1929 and the Great Forest Fires ..................... 41
4. The Year 1930 and the Northern Region Packers' Contest .. 69
5. Packing in the Idaho Panhandle .................................. 79
6. Working in Glacier National Park ............................... 97
7. The Ptarmigan Tunnel Story ..................................... 111
8. The Bar-X-Six Story .............................................. 117
9. On the East Side of Glacier National Park .................. 129
10. Sun Camp and the Two Bears ................................. 151
11. Postwar Years at Grand Canyon ............................. 159
12. Back at Glacier .................................................. 173

During his half-century career, William J. Yenne (1908–1994) came to be widely recognized as the most accomplished and knowledgeable outdoorsman who ever rode the backcountry of Glacier National Park. Mel Ruder, the Pulitzer Prize–winning founder of the *Hungry Horse News*, who accompanied W.J. Yenne on many of his backcountry inspection tours, called him "the man who best knows Glacier National Park's one thousand miles of trails."

# FOREWORD

If I could have ridden ten thousand miles of mountain trails with Bill Yenne it wouldn't have been enough, but I'm thankful for the few hundred we did ride together and the campfires we shared. They weren't all sunny days, but even a tough one wasn't so bad when sharing adventure with the top hand.

Bill Yenne might have been the best packer to ever throw a diamond hitch or pull a string of mules over the Continental Divide in a blizzard. He was a charter member of the "Wild Bunch" and their guest each year at the National Finals Rodeo. Bill remembered more cowboy lore, famous horses and riders, winners and losers than anyone I ever knew. He dressed immaculately, with mustache trimmed, and was never seen unshaven. It was fundamental that all stock in his string were saddled and packed in showcase style.

Bill was a proud and kindly man, a teacher of youth and an unequalled wilderness guide. He was also a sophisticated world traveler, but when he put on that Stetson hat, climbed aboard his horse and started spinning a high country yarn, his listeners didn't know if he'd ever been south of Belton.

Above everything else, he was the consummate western storyteller. The topic didn't matter. You could ask either an intelligent question or a dumb one and then settle back because a fantastic tale was coming your way.

With disarming ease, he laced his stories with names, dates and tiny details, all of which established unquestionable authenticity. He related each story with a sincerity and force, absolutely defying you to not believe every single word. He set you up, and in the end, he lowered the boom. My trying to tell one of Bill's stories is a fool's game, but somebody has to do it.

It was late August 1966. Bill was guiding three government big shots and one *Hungry Horse* columnist on a saddle horse trip over Glacier Park's Boulder Pass during a snowstorm. In the rocks above the Hole in the Wall Basin, we found a young woman in distress. She and the rest of a geology class from the University of Michigan had lost the trail. She didn't know where the others were and was suffering from hypothermia. Bill told her to stay put while he and I found the others. Visibility was zilch, but we rounded them all up, told them to stick right behind one another and follow us.

Few of that Michigan group were equipped for the snow, but walking warmed them up. At a little lake a mile below Brown's Pass, we broke out of bad weather, built a friendly fire for warmth and coffee and soon had them in good spirits. Then one of the students innocently asked, "Mr. Yenne, do many people break the rules and take home a rock from Glacier Park?"

Bill tips the brim of his hat back with a thumb, gazes out over the awesome collection of towering peaks and ten zillion rocks and then says, "Not often, but that sort of thing does happen now and then. Only five years back there was a lady out here from Philadelphia or one of those big eastern seaports, and just up there on the south side of Mount Chapman [Bill motions to the north] she picked up a pretty rock, wasn't a big one, around half a pound as I recall, kinda reddish color with a white streak through it.

"Anyway, she put it in her pack and carried it down to Goat Haunt and, with the innocence of a lamb, illegally smuggled it into Canada on the Waterton Ferry—then doggone if she didn't smuggle it back into the United States in a bus over Chief Mountain Road. I recall she was a school marm about 41 or 42 years old. Well sir! Later that winter, back in the far east, she gets to readin' the literature of her vacation out here and comes to that part where it says visitors cannot remove anything from Glacier National Park.

"Lucky for us, this lady was a Christian and knew she had sinned, so she gets that rock off the mantle, wraps it in a lot of excelsior and mails it in a padded box to Park Headquarters. I was gone that day checking on horses at Perma, but others say the Superintendent and the Chief Naturalist were both excited when that package came, even debated over who should sign for it. They convened a special panel and called in consulting geologists, including the renowned Ned Barrow from Yellowstone, to make sure it was one of our rocks.

"During the next full-staff meeting on April 12th, it was decided that because I had been in Glacier longer than anyone else, I should be in charge of that rock."

Bill pauses here and looks out over the great expanse of towering peaks. Then, shaking his head in disbelief and in a voice filled with humble emotion, he speaks, "I was touched by the faith placed in me, but I'll tell you folks the truth. As well as I know this Park, it was into August before I figured out where that rock fit."

It's sort of fun for me to think of Bill up there at the Big Corral in the Sky hunkered down in his chaps and swappin' yarns with Mark Twain, Charlie Russell and Will Rogers.

He'll hold his own.

—GEORGE OSTROM

*George Ostrom has been a popular commentator in northwestern Montana and the Flathead Valley since the 1950s. He built his* Kalispell Weekly News *into the largest circulation weekly newspaper in Montana. His "Trailwatcher" column won first place from the National Newspaper Association in 1996. He has hosted radio and television programs, authored several books and continues to lead hikes with the "Over-the-Hill Gang" in Glacier Park and the surrounding area. In 2003, he was inducted into the Montana Broadcasters Hall of Fame, and in 2006, he received the University of Montana Distinguished Alumni Award.*

William J. Yenne standing next to his favorite roan horse at Triple Divide Pass, with Mount James in the background, on August 11, 1962. From left to right, the mounted riders are Glacier National Park chief naturalist Francis Elmore, Ranger Charles A. "Chuck" Budge and the author's twelve-year-old son, William P. Yenne. Triple Divide marks the intersection of the Continental Divide and the Hudson Bay Divide. The author's 1995 memorial commemoration took place on this spot.

# INTRODUCTION

hrough the years, it has been a source of immense pride to have crossed paths with so many people who have recognized my father, William J. Yenne, as the most accomplished and knowledgeable outdoorsman who ever rode the backcountry of Glacier National Park. Mel Ruder, the Pulitzer Prize–winning founder of the *Hungry Horse News*, who accompanied him on many of his backcountry inspection tours, called him "the man who best knows Glacier National Park's one thousand miles of trails." During my younger years, up through my early teens, I was along on many of these trips and was gradually getting a sense from the people who accompanied us of how highly regarded he was, even by the highest ranking of National Park Service officials

Through the 1950s and 1960s, his work for the U.S. National Park Service took him on virtually every trail in Glacier, nearly every year. He knew each mile of those trails intimately and could identify every mountain peak and every glacier at a glance. He was also a renowned storyteller. Those who remember him recall him both for travels shared in the Glacier backcountry and for his amusing and fascinating yarns, spun around campfires and kitchen tables, many of which are preserved in this book. In addition to all the stories as he wrote them in 1983, the final chapter of this edition is augmented by stories that I transcribed from a lecture he gave at Lake McDonald Lodge in August 1985, as well as from his correspondence with friends later in that decade.

In addition to his campfire tales, W.J. Yenne was a master of the witty retort. One incident, often retold, involved his being asked about glacial moraine, the rocks strewn across a valley in the high country by glaciers during the ice age of the Cenozoic Era.

"Where did all these rocks come from?" he was asked.

"The glacier brought them," he replied, truthfully.

"Where is the glacier now?"

"It went back for more rocks," he said authoritatively, but with a wry smile.

Mel Ruder described him as having "the lean look of a man who spends many hours in the saddle. A good outdoorsman, he presents the clean-shaven scrubbed look. His physical condition is better than many men half his age, and his dedication to Glacier's trails, a wonder to behold."

W.J. Yenne was born on the family homestead near Creston, Montana, about thirty miles from Glacier, on August 4, 1908. After having ridden in rodeos professionally while in his teens, he began working for the federal government in 1928 as a packer for Blackfeet National Forest, now a part of the Flathead National Forest. He was also a packer in St. Joe and Clearwater National Forests in Idaho before joining the National Park Service in Glacier in 1932. Following World War II, he was a foreman on Glacier's trails, and from 1948 to 1951, he headed trail maintenance in Grand Canyon National Park, where I was born. After we returned to Glacier, he spent nearly two decades as Trails Supervisor, with the dual responsibility of Roads Supervisor for much of that time. As Mel Ruder pointed out, he was also "an effective Park Safety Director." It was during those years that I spent much time in the outdoors with him.

During the 1960s, his work with the National Park Service took him far beyond the mountains of the West—from the Stephen Mather Center at Harpers Ferry to Bettles Field, north of the Arctic Circle in Alaska, where he led a major firefighting effort. He was a friend of U.S. Senator Max Baucus of Montana. In the 1970s and early 1980s, he guided Baucus on trips throughout the Glacier backcountry and visited the senator at his office in Washington, D.C., several times.

In addition to the original edition of Switchback, published in 1983, he also authored several other books during these years, including Wildlife of North America (1984) and The Pictorial Encyclopedia of Horses (1989).

My father's reputation as a horseman and as a historian spread nationally. The National Cowboy and Western Heritage Museum named him as a charter and lifetime member of its Rodeo Historical Society, as well as of the Rodeo Hall of Fame "Wild Bunch."

After his retirement from the U.S. National Park Service in 1969, my father returned to Glacier nearly every summer for two decades, where he worked as a guide with the saddle horse concessionaire in the Park, while also guiding for the Park Service and the U.S. Geologic Survey. Meanwhile, he worked as a packer and guide in the adjacent Bob Marshall Wilderness Area. In his later years, he taught horse packing classes in the Northwest and worked special assignments for the National Park Service in Yosemite National Park. As Mel Ruder wrote, "He was still saddling horses when he was 81 years old."

William J. Yenne died on September 24, 1994, in Capitola, California. In accordance with his final wishes that his memorial service occur in the high country of Glacier, it was held the following summer at Triple Divide Pass. For this trip, I was accompanied by my daughter (and his granddaughter) Annalisa Yenne, as well as his nephew, Gerald Yenne, and four of his longtime friends: Art Burch, Art Burch Jr., Bill Orr and Bill Wendt.

—WILLIAM P. YENNE

*After growing up in Glacier National Park, W.P. Yenne graduated from the University of Montana and went on to a long and ongoing career as an award-winning author, historian and novelist. He has appeared in numerous documentaries on the History Channel, Smithsonian Channel and the National Geographic Channel. Surrounded by remarkable children and grandchildren, he and his wife live in San Francisco. His own story unfolds at www.billyenne.com.*

The Yenne Farm (formerly the O'Leary Homestead) north of Creston, Montana, in 1917.

The Yenne family in February 1917. Their mother, Mary Ethel "Minnie" O'Leary Yenne, is on the left, holding Ann, the youngest daughter. Peter Samuel Yenne is the tall man in the back. From left to right are the Yenne children, Ann, Florence, Clyde and Tom, with Art Weaver, who boarded with the family around this time. William J. Yenne is on the far right.

## Chapter 1

# EARLY DAYS IN THE UPPER FLATHEAD LAKE COUNTRY

I was born and grew up on a farm near Creston, ten miles east of Kalispell, Montana, in an area that was then known as the Jessup Mill area. Herb Jessup had built flour and sawmills there after damming the flow of some giant freshwater springs. It had been known that the water from these springs and, after the dam was built, the pond varied only slightly in temperature from the coldest winter to the warmest summer and that the volume of the flow remained constant year-round. In later years, my father became a one-fourth owner of this property, and in the late 1930s, this property was purchased by the U.S. Department of the Interior for the purpose of building a large fish hatchery there.

The farm where I was born was the homestead of my maternal grandparents, Dennis and Margaret O'Leary. They were among the first dozen families to settle in the Upper Flathead Valley. [Editor's note: A copy of the document conveying title of the 160 acres of his homestead to Dennis O'Leary, dated December 14, 1895, and signed personally in two places by President Grover Cleveland, is still in the possession of the family. So, too, is the acreage of the original homestead. Title to a homestead came as a confirmation that the homesteader had successfully established and worked the land for five years.]

Although my father's parents did not arrive from Kansas until a few years later, three of my father's uncles, all millwrights, had come to the valley in the 1880s. They built sawmills and flour mills and were known to have made the first white flour made in northwestern Montana. Their ads in the

The old Yenne home as it appears today. Members of the family have lived here for more than a century. *Azia Yenne.*

newspapers of the time tell of their being able to make moldings in their planer mills that equaled any that could be shipped in.

One of the brothers, my father's uncle Jesse Yenne, established a homestead on a peninsula at the northeast corner of Flathead Lake near what is now Bigfork. Jess Yenne was the first (or at least one of the two first) to grow sweet cherries on the shores of Flathead Lake, which is today an important cherry growing region. His orchard was known as "Yenne Point Orchard." The site of his orchard is known as Yenne Point to this day.

My father, Pete Yenne, like most of the farmers and ranchers of the area, raised all of his own horses, as well as many to sell. These horses were not of the heavy draft breeds, but rather the saddle breed, the Hambletonian type crossbred with Morgan. Just about any of our horses you could select would serve very well as a saddle horse. They also were all good "buggy horses" or "cutter horses" for winter. They served very well as draft horses, although on heavier draft loads more horses were needed.

In the discipline of horse handling, my dad was a good teacher. We learned how to halter break young horses and to break them to ride and to the harness. We learned how to approach an animal likely to kick or one likely to become nervous and skittish or hard to catch. This training served me well in qualifying for rodeo riding and later for my first job with the Forest Service.

Our neighbors had a lot of medium-sized work horses that had never been ridden. Some of them were pretty well blooded and pretty feisty. The neighbors were after my two brothers and me to ride these horses and to see how much they could buck. When I was about twelve years old, my brother Tom, about a year and a half younger, and my brother Clyde, who was about four years older, started riding them. They weren't too interested in it, but I got the rodeo fever.

By the time I was sixteen, I could work the bigger rodeos. I was still a farmer boy, but I could ride a tougher horse than some of these guys who were following the rodeo circuit. I found that I could make considerable spending money riding in the local rodeos at places like Columbia Falls, Kalispell, Elmo, Hot Springs and Polson. Later, I rodeoed farther afield. While still in my teens I rode two horses at the Pendleton Roundup in Oregon. At some of those rodeos where horses were in surplus and riders scarce I have ridden a half dozen or more broncs in an afternoon. In the

The Yenne and Eccles Mill on Lang Creek southeast of Kalispell in August 1890. Left to right are Robert Gatiss, Oscar Olson, John Eccles, Jess Yenne, Ed Tristad and Joseph Eccles Sr. *Matt Eccles*.

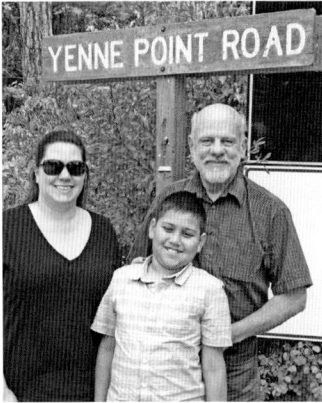

The author's granddaughter Azia Yenne; his great-grandson Cash Bolos; and his son, William P. Yenne, at Yenne Point in 2016. *Mike Bolos*.

area southwest of Flathead Lake, near where I grew up, there were several ranchers who owned good bucking horses. They, along with rodeo producers like Roy Enochs and Charlie Prongie, were the ones who furnished the stock for those local rodeos.

Fights, of course, were common at rodeos. I recall riding in the rodeo at Conrad, Montana, and while there seeing one of the best bare fist fights I have ever seen.

I was with Dick Michels, with whom I was traveling and rodeoing, and had a ringside seat atop a bucking chute when it took place. The night before, several men had pointed out to us a man nicknamed "Powder River" and told us that he was as tough a fighting man as there was in the state. He was nearly six feet tall, weighed about 200 pounds and many said he could knock a man down easier than any they had ever seen. Dick and I were each about eighteen at the time, and after hearing again how this man could fight, Dick said to me, "Let's flip a coin to see which of us challenges him."

At this rodeo were two part-Indian brothers, Marion and Louie Salios, who were also entered in the riding events. Louie sort of took Dick and me under his wing and helped us when we were getting the rigging on our mounts in the chute and in getting mounted. He asked us if we were entered in the saddle bronc riding. I said I was. In those days, the "Association" or committee saddles, the standard event saddle still used in the saddle bronc event in all rodeos today, were generally furnished by the town putting on the rodeo. The Conrad Rodeo saddles were brand new and were hard and slippery as varnished furniture. Louie had an Association saddle of his own that he had used for a year and which was well broken in, and he said I was welcome to use it when I rode the horses I had drawn. Dick and I commented several times what a fine fellow this Louie was.

On the last day of the rodeo, Powder River and Louie got into an argument over the saddle bronc Louie had drawn. Powder River claimed that he should have that horse, a showy bucker with no nasty habits, the kind that riders like to draw. Our perch was just above them when Powder threw his first punch at Louie. During the three minutes of that fight (about the length of a round in boxing) Powder hardly landed a good punch. At the

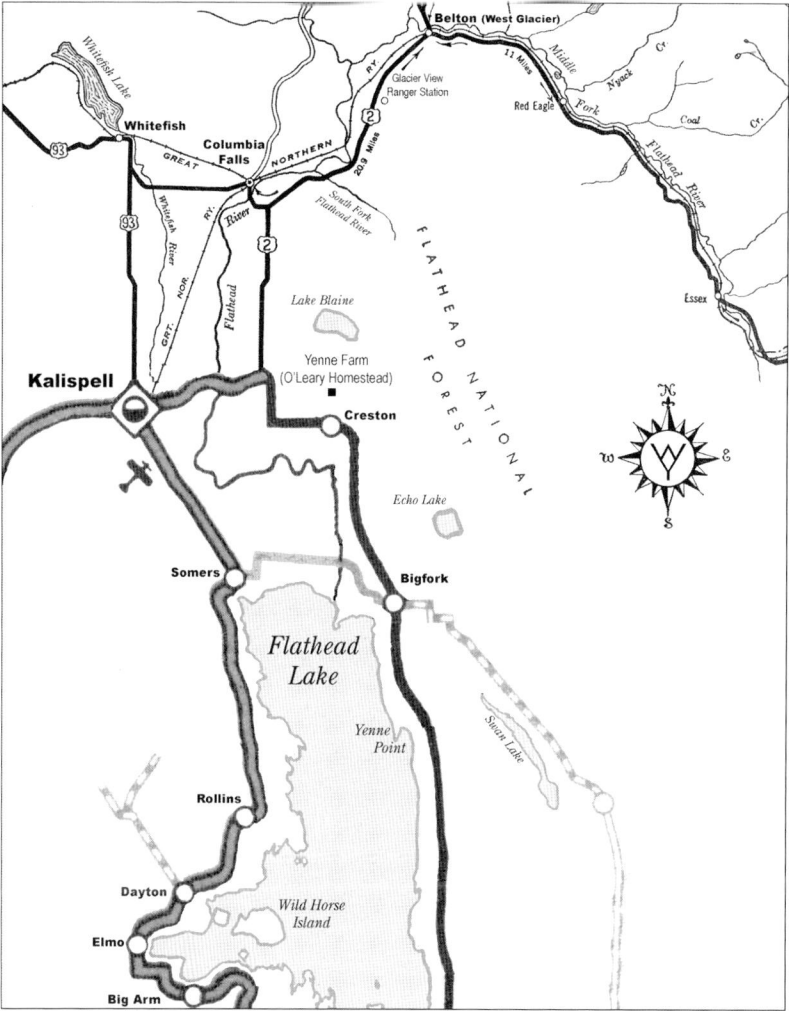

This map of the Upper Flathead Lake Country shows the location of the Yenne Farm in relation to the southern edge of Glacier National Park (*top*), Kalispell (the Flathead County seat) and Flathead Lake. On the east side of Flathead Lake, note Yenne Point, where Jess Yenne had his cherry orchard.

end he was on his hands and knees with blood dripping from his face into the dust. I talked with Louie later and asked him about his training. He said he had learned at an Indian school.

In the backcountry along the forks of the Flathead River, the Forest Service was in the process of building ranger stations, patrol cabins, lookout cabins and many bridges, as well as trails and telephone lines. Tons of building materials, food and camping equipment were being packed to the crews in the backcountry. Pack strings usually consisted of two men with their saddle horses and twelve pack horses. The old sawbuck packsaddle was still in use, but in the forests of northern Idaho the Decker brothers had invented another type of packsaddle that was easier and simpler to pack. It was much easier on the animal's back since the saddle tree was made of thick cottonwood and could be rasped to fit the back of the animal that was to wear it. The tree of the old sawbuck packsaddle was made of hardwood, and lucky was the animal whose back happened to fit the saddle cinched to his back.

By about 1924, the forests of western Montana had gradually started to adapt to the Decker saddle and to the use of mules instead of horses as pack animals. Oliver P. Robinette of Kooskia was the blacksmith who almost from the beginning had made all of the Decker packsaddle trees. Robinette built the trees to their specification and then continued to build them. He always burned his initials on each tree bar, which he made of cottonwood. The OPR brand on a tree was indeed a symbol of excellence. To this day, among the big game outfitters, Decker trees branded OPR can still be found. The large Flathead National Forest had bought a number of mules from the John Cervant ranch of Malta, Montana. Another string of mules was needed up in the smaller Blackfeet National Forest to the north on the Whitefish Divide, so the Flathead Forest sold eight of their newly acquired mules to them. Four of these mules had proven to be hard for the Flathead packers to handle. This was early fall 1927, and before the end of the work season two successive packers had quit rather than try to handle those mules. They were said to be kickers, would bite their handler if opportunity presented, were hard to catch, did not lead well and were head shy, thus hard to halter.

That winter a ranger named S.L. (Samuel Louis) McNelly was transferred from the Deer Lodge National Forest to the Glacier View (North Fork of the Flathead River) district of the Blackfeet Forest. In the spring he hired a packer who had packed for him in the Deer Lodge. The man lasted a little more than two weeks. When he left, he told others of the crew that life was too short to have to take that punishment.

When he left, Ranger McNelly called all of the men together and asked them if they knew of a man that they thought could handle that stock. He said it was embarrassing to have those mules run three packers off, that they were stuck with them and that there was a tremendous amount of packing to

W.J. Yenne was riding saddle broncs professionally at numerous rodeos in his late teens.

be done. One of the men, Harry Jessup, who had known me all my life, told McNelly he knew a man who could. McNelly said, "Are you sure?" Harry said, "Yes, he can handle them."

I was in eastern Montana at the time on a rodeoing trip. When I got home, a letter from the Forest Service was awaiting me offering me the packing job. I phoned the supervisor's office in Kalispell and told them I'd take the job. The forest supervisor told me that a truck from the Glacier View district in the North Fork was in town, that if I would come to the forest service warehouse my papers would be there for me to fill out and sign and I could then ride up to the ranger station with the truck.

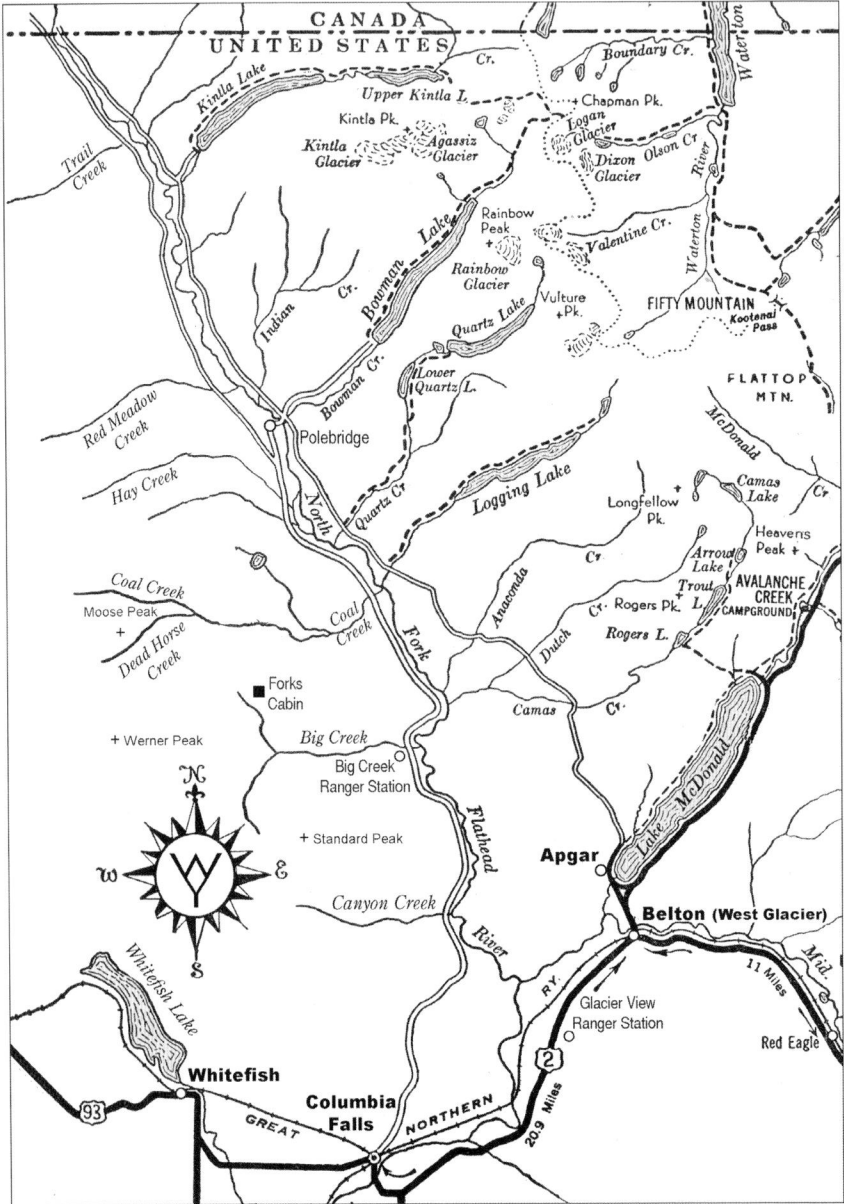

The North Fork Country is bisected diagonally by the North Fork of the Flathead River, with Glacier National Park to the east and U.S. Forest Service land to the west. The latter area was designated as the Blackfeet National Forest in July 1908. In June 1935, the Blackfeet was divided between the Flathead and Kootenai National Forests, and the name was discontinued. The area seen here west of the North Fork has been part of the Flathead National Forest since.

*Chapter 2*

# PACKING AND TRAIL BUILDING ON THE NORTH FORK OF THE FLATHEAD RIVER

At the Forest Service warehouse I learned that the driver of the truck that was to take me to my newfound job on the North Fork was Harry Jessup, the man who had recommended me. After I filled out the government forms necessary for my employment, we were on our way.

Jobs were not plentiful in those days for men who weren't war veterans and had no dependents, so I recognized my good fortune to fill one of the higher paying jobs. I vowed to myself that I would not let them down. A year later I was the highest paid packer in the forest.

Upon my arrival at the Glacier View Ranger Station, I was shown around by Ralph Reichert, the ranger alternate, and Jerry Dahl, the commissary clerk. In no time I was at the barn and corrals inspecting the saddles, pads and other gear necessary for use by a pack string. I checked the fences, the hay and grain on hand and took a stroll around the surrounding area. The packsaddles were of the Decker type with the trees of the OPR brand.

Before long, the strawberry roan bell mare came to the corral, followed by the extra saddle horses, "Paddy" the 1,600-pound draft horse and the eight big mules. I had already filled the nosebags I had been able to wangle from Joe Steppler, the supply man at the Kalispell warehouse. The first thing a good packer thinks of is seeing to it that his animals are fed. In doing so I learned just how head shy those mules were. I knew that using nosebags for feeding was the most direct way to cure this bad habit.

A tall bay and white pinto horse was to be my principal mount. Ranger McNelly had two good saddle horses of his own. One, named Sam, was a beautiful liver chestnut with a perfect quarter horse build. I will be telling much more later about Sam, who I shall always remember as one of the four best mountain horses I ever rode.

It was a Thursday or a Friday when I entered on duty as a Forest Service packer. There were to be no pack trips until Monday, so I had a few days to get acquainted with the ranger station routine. The trail building program had fallen behind the past two years, as emphasis had been put on building a fine warehouse and new ranger's residence. Consequently, I would be having a busy season putting trail and telephone line construction crews out to their locations and supplying them. Next, there was the lumber for the new Standard Mountain lookout and the Forks of Big Creek cabin to be packed. Following that fire season, those who manned the fire lookouts would be sent to their summer stations and supplied.

Many times during these next days before Monday Ranger McNelly asked me if I thought I would be able to handle the stock. Each time I assured him that I could but would add that there were a "few" things I did not know about packing. I realized later that he was aware that there were a lot of things I didn't know about packing. Each time I told him this, he would say, "Don't worry about that. If you need any pointers I can help you. What we need most here is a man that can handle that stock." Again I would assure him that he had nothing to fear along that line.

During the summer fire season, the ranger station received routine reports on conditions from all the lookouts. From the west side of the Whitefish Divide, Olney, Stryker, Trego and Fortine would come reports morning and afternoon daily. Among the men issuing the reports were Maurice Cusick, Pete DeGroot and Fred Herrig. Fred Herrig, who was very much respected by all who knew him, was a tall, well-proportioned man of above average height and size. He had been formally retired from the Forest Service only the year before (1927), and I had the pleasure of seeing and talking with him several times when he came up into the North Fork area to visit old haunts and friends. On more than one occasion, when a mutual friend would start to introduce us, Fred would tell when and where he had previously talked with me.

Fred Herrig, earlier in his career, had punched cattle for Theodore Roosevelt at the latter's ranch in North Dakota. He and Roosevelt became very close personal friends, and when Teddy was organizing his famous Rough Riders, he sent word to Fred Herrig, who was at the time packing ore in British Columbia, to come to San Antonio and join up. Fred did so and subsequently distinguished himself to a great extent at San Juan Hill.

At one point during Fred's tenure with Roosevelt's Rough Riders, he tracked down and recovered a string of mules loaded with machine guns that had got away during a skirmish and which several full-blood Indians had been unsuccessful in locating.

While a ranger at Kintla Lake in Glacier National Park, Fred met, wooed and won an attractive widow named Mrs. Wilke, who lived in Badrock Canyon. It was about this time that President Roosevelt appointed him a permanent ranger with the U.S. Forest Service and assigned him to the Kootenai National Forest. His station was Ant Flat, west of the Whitefish Divide.

Fred lived in a 12x18-foot log cabin at Ant Flat and patrolled his domain on a magnificent black saddle horse accompanied by his Russian wolf hound, Bruno. Fred's spurs were silver, and his horse wore a silver studded bridle and martingale. He carried a .45-70 rifle in his saddle scabbard and wore a .38 revolver, a gift from his friend President Roosevelt.

Fred was succeeded as ranger at Ant Flat by La Vaugh Beaman in the early 1920s but continued in a lesser capacity with the Forest Service until his retirement in 1927. Fred's stepson, Bert Wilke, was a packer for the Blackfeet Forest at the same time I was and for many years thereafter, retiring in 1958.


THE NORTH FORK ROAD crew was making its headquarters at Big Creek Ranger Station. Harry Pennoyer was the foreman, and Charlie Hollingworth was cooking for the entire crew so there was no batching. The big pack mules had proven to be not much different from the horses I had handled since childhood so that before fall I had broken four of the more tractable ones to the riding saddle. As for the lumber packing, well, the mules and I sort of learned it together. One day, when making a trip to the Forks cabin with a stringload of lumber and shingles, a shingle pack bumped a six-inch lodgepole at the trailside that apparently was waiting for a breath of wind to knock it down. At any rate, it fell across the packsaddle of one of the mules loaded with lumber, knocking him to the ground. He lay there grunting while I chopped the tree off him.

One day, not long after a particularly windy spell, I was to make a trip to Dead Horse Ridge to take supplies to a six-man trail crew and move their camp. Ranger McNelly chose to go with me in order to inspect the section of trail the crew had finished. As we got to within a couple of miles from camp, we came to a "burn" or section of fire-killed timber. This timber had been killed by either the 1910 or 1919 fires. The logs that had fallen across the trail were from six to fourteen inches in diameter and as hard as teak. Both of us had good axes, but by the time we reached the camp we were pretty well done in with all the chopping. I recall that McNelly explained in no uncertain terms to his foreman what he should have done, knowing that the winds that we'd had would have downed those dead trees, and that we were coming with their supplies. After that, when I was due for a trip to that camp, the foreman made sure the trail was thoroughly checked in advance.

Another time, I was to move Art Lynch's camp up on Coal Creek; about that time a fire was reported on the Whitefish Divide near the head of the South Fork of Coal Creek. On this trip to the fire I was riding the bell mare, as I'd had several one-day trips and had not taken her on any of them. Consequently, she was the most rested of the horses, and it was best to have her along because I thought I would probably be turning the mules loose that night. The four-man crew going to the fire had started out from the Forks cabin, and I caught up with them north of and below Werner Peak Lookout. At this point, we felt we should be able to see the smoke from the fire, but as we proceeded northward we failed to spot it. We did a lot of circling for an hour or more when we were fairly certain we had reached the area where the fire had been reported. The four men were getting leg weary by this time, so I found a spot where there was good grass, left the crew to look after the stock while they grazed and hiked the three miles or so back to Werner Peak Lookout.

From there, with the help of the two men stationed there—Lowell Cook, the lookout man, and Millard Evenson, the smokechaser—we were able to locate it. On the way there I had seen four grizzly bears at a distance, a sow with two cubs and a lone grizzly about a mile from them. I got back to the crew, got them to the fire and started to trench it. Then, as I had Art Lynch's camp to move down below the forks of Coal Creek, I decided to make it to his camp that night. I found the trail down the South Fork of Coal Creek without much difficulty. I had to chop out several windfalls, as the trail had not been cleared that year, but when I came to the forks of the creek the trail just ended. Up to that point it had been somewhat a worn and well-used trail and easy to follow. Before I had much time to scout for the trail, it was getting too dark to see the trail even if I came upon it, and it seemed folly to retrace back up that steep trail, so I decided to spend the night right there. I had oats for the stock and nosebags to feed them in, and having had a couple of hours of real good grazing that afternoon, they would not suffer, so I unsaddled them and we spent the night at the forks of the creek in very heavy timber.

The author at Glacier View Ranger Station in the Blackfeet National Forest (later Flathead National Forest).

The next morning, by hiking downstream and crossing a windfall that was across the creek, I found the trail on the north side. I followed it upstream about a quarter of a mile past the forks where my stock were, where it crossed the creek and angled downstream, but uphill, up the ridge and at the top of the ridge I made a sharp switchback. At this point, there was thick snow brush, and apparently game coming down to the creek to drink had, instead of making that switchback, just continued down the ridge to the forks of the creek. This accounted for the plain trail I had followed to the forks of the night before.

At this time, there were three Canadian oil companies, the British Columbia, Glacier and Crows Nest, operating in British Columbia, immediately north of us. Ira and Merle Cassidy were two brothers who worked for the British Columbia Oil Company that we all got to know well. One day, Ira and his wife stopped by the station on their way to Columbia Falls, and he showed us the hides of five grizzlies he had shot at their garbage dump a couple of nights

31

before, with the help of his wife and a five-cell flashlight. She had stood behind him and shone the light along the rifle barrel.

By that time I had learned that different families of grizzlies usually have distinctive coloring. All of these hides were a blue, mouse color. In later years, after I started working across the river in Glacier National Park, I saw many grizzlies of the same color at and near the Doverspike homestead just south of Kintla Creek.

One evening at Big Creek station, I was across the creek at the barn and corrals and just starting to cross the foot-log toward the station when a car drove in with Ralph Thayer in it. As he was getting out of the car, I could see that Ralph could scarcely move one of his legs. He had been up on the southern end of the Whitefish Divide locating trail (a trail, the building of which was contracted the next year) and was in snow brush nearly five feet high. He had heard a commotion and a sound like a bear climbing a tree, had taken a good look and saw a good-sized grizzly bear coming toward him. He had a 1.5-pound cruiser axe in his right hand, and without relinquishing his hold on it, he started to climb the nearest tree. He didn't get far, though, as the bear arrived and fastened her teeth in his thigh. He had his right arm around the tree with the axe still in his hand. He put his left thumb in the corner of her mouth and proceeded to gouge her eye with his finger.

This proved somewhat effective because she loosened her hold on his thigh and dropped to all fours. Ralph took advantage of this brief respite and managed to lunge a few feet farther up the tree, but not quite out of her reach. This time she raised up on her hind legs and sank her teeth into the calf of his leg. He was wearing a pair of calked Bergman loggers shoes, so hanging to the tree with both arms, he proceeded to slash the bear's face with the calked boot of his free foot. Again the bear dropped to all fours, but as she did, her teeth caught the top of his boot and literally pulled him out of the tree. As the bear came down on all fours, he landed on his back on her back. He rolled over, landing on his feet, and it flashed through his mind what old trappers had told him about trapped grizzlies: you could literally chop their heads to pieces and they'd keep coming, but a sharp blow across the snout would temporarily stun them. Therefore, he hit the grizzly across the snout with the flat side of the double bit cruiser axe. I asked him if he had the axe in both hands when he hit her, and he said, "Hell, yes, and both feet off the ground!"

While the grizzly was regaining her composure, Ralph did a good job of climbing another tree a short distance away. He waited in his tree until she got her cubs to the ground and sauntered away before he came down out of his tree. At that time Ralph was one of the best hikers I knew of, but it took him six hours to hike the ten miles down to the North Fork Road at Canyon Creek, where he caught this ride to Big Creek. Ranger McNelly took him to Kalispell in his yellow Buick convertible, which was about as fast an automobile as there was on the road at that time. I don't know how long he was in the hospital, but I seem to recall that he was back on the job eleven days later and ready to finish locating the seventeen-mile trail. Millard Evenson was sent out with him to help him finish the job, and I packed their camp up Canyon Creek to the location that Ralph had picked out and stayed all night with them. When I started back to Big Creek the next morning, after getting a date from them on which I would come to pack them out, I noticed that each of them was armed with a hunting rifle and a large-caliber revolver.

When I came back a few days later to pack them out, they were already in camp. When they started telling me how short they had run on groceries, I reminded them that I had told them when I'd packed them in that I thought they had shorted themselves even though they had a whole warehouse full of groceries to draw from. For supper about all we had was baking powder pancakes, and so help me, I think we even had Farina with canned milk. We bickered a little about the groceries, and after taking my stock up the trail a distance and turning them loose on a grassy slide, I came back to supper. They were still giving me a bad time in a good-natured sort of way, so when I saw what they had fixed for supper I said, "Hell fellows, I've already *had* breakfast." We kept at each other this way the rest of the evening. I think the reason for them keeping at me was their feeling so good about their having finished a tough job.

The next morning, when I had gotten my stock in, fed and saddled, Thayer and Evenson had rolled their beds and were preparing our breakfast. I hardly dared to look at what the menu was going to be, but my worst fears were realized. They had cooked the last of the Farina (also known as Cream of Wheat). While I watched, Thayer dished it up in three portions. It looked to me like my portion was the largest, and I told them so. A debate ensued, with my protesting that it would be impossible for me to eat that much Farina. Finally, both of them picked up their .45-caliber revolvers and pointed them in my direction and suggested that I ought to eat it. Going along with the act, I ate my Farina while they took turns at threatening me with a wave of their guns.

Ralph Thayer was a woodsman who was highly respected by all of his peers. During his lengthy service with the Forest Service, and after his retirement, his

*Left*: The Standard Mountain Lookout in the Blackfeet National Forest just after it was completed in 1928.

*Right*: The old Werner Peak Lookout in the Blackfeet National Forest as it appeared in 1928.

name has remained a legend. He was a fast and tireless hiker. He located, or blazed out, the routes of nearly all of the trails in the North Fork, then just named the Glacier View district. When the small Blackfeet Forest was divided, the North Fork of the Flathead River portion was absorbed by the Flathead Forest and Thayer continued his career for the Flathead.

During the horrible fire year of 1929 in the North Fork, Thayer was the principal fire scout for the entire region. He was the first man to every one of the large fires. He located the campsites for the crews that were to follow. He also would blaze or mark with notebook pages the route I was to follow, as I was usually the second man to all of these fires, leading a pack string and followed by fifty to two hundred men. My first trip would be a stringload of food, mess outfits, Kimmel stoves and hand tools such as axes, saws and Pulaski tools. Usually I would also take a Pacific Marine pump, gasoline and suction hoses to be put in the stream or lake and 1,500 feet of one-and-a-half-inch hose.

I wish that I had saved some of those cross checked yellow pages Thayer had torn from his notebook and stuck on a tree branch or a bit of brush with directions for me. All began with my sobriquet, "Farina Kid," that he had hung on me and ended just "Thayer."

BECAUSE OF THE HEAVY workload in pack train transportation that had built up in the district, I was having 150-mile weeks, over 500 trail miles per month. Since a saddle horse is loaded both going and coming, the miles tell on him before the pack animals. Ranger McNelly allowed me to ride his horses so as to alternate with the big pinto assigned to me as my top horse. Sometimes when he felt that Sam needed more exercise, I would use him. I packed Paddy, the draft horse, and sometimes when the pinto was rested and I needed another pack animal, I would pack him. We continued to have the usual number of lightning fires, also an occasional grizzly bear incident. I had encountered many of them, particularly on the Glacier Park and North Fork River side of the Whitefish Divide.

As 1928 was ending, Ranger McNelly began having serious back trouble. I was told that it was the after effect of injuries he had suffered as a motorcycle courier in the army during World War I. Because of the great value the family put on Sam, McNelly asked me if we might winter him at my father's farm instead of having him sent to the Forest Service winter range. This was arranged. By the spring of 1929, it became apparent that McNelly would be unable to continue with his ranger job, so he asked me if I would take Sam and use him as my own horse until he was called for.

In late spring, a packer from the Tally Lake district named Wintras Curtis and I were moving some stock in the Truman Creek area and had occasion to spend the night, or rather two nights, as this was a Saturday, at the camp near Truman Creek of Walt Colby and Carter Hardy. They were both going home, so they turned their camp and all of its new equipment over to us. The tents, stove, tools, dishes and even the blankets were brand new.

After turning the stock loose to roll, we fed them grain in the nosebags we were carrying and set about getting our evening meal. I recall that I had started to peel some potatoes and stopped long enough to go to the spring, some forty yards away, for a bucket of water. As I started back toward the tent, I noticed that, near the shiny new stovepipe, the new, white tent was afire in three places. I yelled to Curtis, who was inside near the stove, also working on our menu. We went to work fighting the blaze, realizing that as we put out the glowing embers in one place in the new canvas, there were a couple of nickel-size spots in another location.

When finally we were sure we had completely extinguished every spark and took the time to look around, we discovered that all of our stock had disappeared up the trail toward Wild Bill Lookout. It had gotten dark by that time, and with the fire still going strong in the cookstove, we dared not leave the camp unattended, so I told Curtis to go ahead with the supper and I took off up the trail, bridle in hand.

Sam was the first animal I caught up with as I trotted up the hill. Each time I called to him he would stop, but as he saw the others ahead of him continuing on, he would go, but at a slower pace. I soon caught up to him and was able to round up all the others but two that had taken to the brush and were impossible to locate in the darkness. The next day, we caught up with them about eight miles beyond the Walt and Charlie Nedreau place in the Hog Heaven country.

The Forest Service also had a team of very large draft mules that were used entirely by the road crew. These animals were wintered south of Columbia Falls by a rancher named Frank Ladenberg because the Forest Service considered them too valuable and too vulnerable to entrust to the winter with its violent storms. During the winter, the smaller of the two had gotten out on the county road and had been struck by a passing truck. It had suffered a broken leg and had to be destroyed. To replace her, we located the largest mule available at the Louie Grob farm at Creston.

On the way up from winter range with the stock, I included the Grob draft mule at Kalispell and upon reaching Columbia Falls put the stock in the railroad stock yards, where hay had been delivered. I then went to the Frank Ladenberg farm and brought the larger work mule to Jim Everin's blacksmith shop for shoeing. This shop was a favorite hangout for the logging teamsters of the area, and when I arrived with the big mule, Steve Quimby, Homer Huggins, Eli Brunett, Jack Gorton and two or three others were gathered there swapping horse talk. The mule I led in was fat and his coat shiny. When inside the shop he looked much larger than he had outdoors. The horse talk came to an end, and all started sizing the mule up with the critical eye of the horseman and horse trader.

After a few minutes, one of the men asked me what the mule would weigh. Without hesitation I said, "1,400." There was an immediate storm of protest from all there, including Jim Everin. None of their estimates were less than 1,550, and at least one was 1,650. They were all trying to talk at once, explaining to each other why a mule would weigh more than a horse of comparable size-bone structure, more solid than a horse, etc. I found myself wishing that I had kept my mouth shut or had at least said I didn't know. 1,400, however, was my own honest guess, and while I never had an opportunity to see any mules weighed, I had been around live and dressed beef and pork all my early life and knew how they affected the scales. A mule does not have the square quarters of a heavy horse, and I'm sure I unconsciously took that into consideration. Now all these expert horsemen had me doubting myself and wondering why I had committed myself. After the shoeing, we took it to the city scales a block away, where it weighed 1,395 pounds.

Jack Lillevig took over as ranger in McNelly's place at the start of the summer of 1929. The 1929 season proved to be about as busy a season for me as any one packer ever had. In the district were two ten-man trail construction crews, two six-man and some four-man crews, two telephone line construction gangs and then came the "Gyppo," or contract crew to build the seventeen-mile Whitefish Divide trail that Thayer had been locating when attacked by the mother grizzly. A group of North Forkers headed by Austin Weikert had got the contract to build this trail from Werner Peak to the South Fork of Canyon Creek. All they were to furnish was the labor. The Forest Service furnished the tools, all camp equipment and all groceries. They just ordered the food they wanted and it was sent to them. One would think that in those days this would be a risky clause, but the Service lost nothing on these men's meals. They ordered the most ordinary staple groceries, and there was no waste. Also, the way they worked it reduced the number of days the Forest Service was to feed them to the barest minimum.

The one clause in the contract that really worked a hardship for poor old busy me was that they were not to have to walk more than two miles to their work. In other words, as soon as they had built two miles of trail, they were to be moved. Since all of this trail was from nineteen to twenty-eight miles distant from Big Creek Station, a camp move was a two-day job. With all my other work, including packing the components for a couple of buildings, those two days could really put me behind schedule in my other packing. This Gyppo crew, however, did all they could to help me and our respective schedules. Each time I moved them, Austin would walk ahead of me past the end of their constructed trail, and we would "bushwhack" as much as two miles before setting up camp. This way they could work both ways from their camp, making their moves less frequent.

In order to rest my stock as much as possible, I would figure out ways of working in any extra stock that might be in the district. I would rest the bell mare when I had one day trips and would often use her as my saddle horse on two-day trips, thus giving Sam a rest. Also, Jack Lilliveg, the new ranger, liked to have his horse, Murphy, ridden at least one or two days a week, and his work kept him at the station most of the time. Murphy had been an exhibition bucking horse when owned by the Bar-X-Six in Glacier Park and could become a bit snuffy if not used regularly. I was the only one other than Jack permitted to ride him, and of course, with my overworked stock, I was happy to oblige. When I made short string trips to lookouts, any extra saddle horses that had not been working found themselves under a packsaddle. Even with this, my regular string was making more than five hundred miles a month.

Before we get too far from Austin Weikert, I'd like to move ahead some twenty-eight years to 1957. That year, Austin was given a contract by the National Park Service in Glacier to build two log shelter cabins. One, the Oastler Shelter, would be put at the head of Josephine Lake and the other, the Judge Pray Shelter, at the head of Two Medicine Lake. Each was where trails connect with boat landings and are for the shelter of those returning from hikes and waiting for launches.

Austin built both of these buildings at Park Headquarters, and it was the job of my crews and I to disassemble them, haul them to the foot of their respective lakes, raft the logs to the head of the lake and erect the building as Austin had originally constructed it. We put in the concrete foundations while Austin was notching the logs and building the shelters. Then I serial numbered the logs as to sides and height, or "round," of each. In each case, when the day came to actually put up the cabin, or shelter, we left Park Headquarters at six in the morning and had the building up, including rafters, by four that afternoon. The roofplanks and roofing were put on later. The day we put up the one at Josephine Lake, a party of four or five older men came by just as we arrived at the site, and I waved a greeting to them as they started up the trail on their all-day hike.

As mentioned, we finished putting the rafters on just before four o'clock and were burning the last of scraps and debris when the hikers we had seen that morning returned from their hike to Morning Eagle Falls. They were absolutely astonished to see a completed log building where there had been nothing a few hours before. Of course, that forenoon they had not noticed that the logs had been notched and grooved. They told of having lived in areas where many log buildings were built and had known

The author with a pack string at the Standard Mountain lookout in 1929.

that a "round a day" was considered standard by log men. Each of the logs had been scribed and grooved so as to fit perfectly the log below it. Austin had not left a crack of one-eighth inch in the grooves or corners.

They examined it minutely in awe. Of course, I had to kid around a little before I told them just how we had accomplished this magic. One thing I told them was that when Austin built a winter snowshoe cabin for winter patrols, we would subject the finished building to a 15-pound air test before we would accept it and pay him. Even after I told them all about how we had done this, they were loud in their praise for all of us.

The town of Belton, at the west entrance of Glacier National Park, survived the fire of 1929, but the nearby towns of Coram and Apgar were mostly destroyed. The fire swept across the mountain seen here in the background.

The Belton Chalets were built by the Great Northern Railway and operated by it from 1910 to 1943. After decades of disrepair, the chalets have been restored to their former glory. The roofs of these buildings are visible at the bottom of the photo at the top.

## Chapter 3

# THE YEAR 1929 AND
# THE GREAT FOREST FIRES

When Jack Lillevig had a chance to get out in the field to explore his new district, he liked to go where I was going, which was the case with most officials because then they had no livestock worries. Their stock would be turned out with the pack string, and the packer would gather them in the next morning. When I packed the supplies to Werner Peak for the lookout man and smokechaser, Jack went along for his first look at that part of the country. The lookout man, Paul Martin, and the smokechaser, Dave Stimson, had hiked from the Forks Cabin, maintaining telephone line as they went.

That night, Jack and I made our beds on the floor while Paul and Dave occupied the two cots. My bed was hard, making it difficult to get to sleep at once. As I lay there, I could hear a scuffing, rustling noise on the ridge to the south where my saddles were stacked. I had been lying perfectly still so as not to disturb Jack, but now I quietly raised up for a look out the large windows at my head. As soon as I moved, Jack, who had also been having trouble going to sleep, said, "What do you see?" in a whisper. It was moonlight out there, and I could see a porcupine near the saddles, and told Jack so. Without hesitation, he said, "Let's go get him," and crawled out of his blankets. He slipped on his cowboy boots, which were equipped with steel heel plates, while I put on an old pair of oxfords I usually carried along on two-day trips. Pulling two detachable shovel handles from the smokechaser packs, we gave chase to the porky. Before we could get close enough to get in a telling blow, he turned off the ridge to the westward, over an area of sloping solid rock.

As soon as Jack's steel heel plates came into contact with this smooth, solid rock, his feet flew out from under him and he went sliding over the rock on his backside.

Needless to say, the porcupine escaped and Jack didn't, bleeding from the contact with the rock surface. Back in the lookout, I lit a candle to assist in finding the first-aid materials and was performing my first aid, Jack bending over the table with his shorts down at his boots, when the two others woke up. I remember Stimson saying, "What in hell are you guys doing?"

Another time that Jack went with me was on a trip to Moose Lake and Moose Peak. I was packing lumber to the peak, where Johnny Glover was building a lookout cabin, but staying the night at the lake, where a small telephone line crew was camped. Jack had taken a side trip at Kletomas Creek and had not gone to the peak with me. The next morning, he said he would like to go to the peak and would like for me to go up with him so we could ride back the nineteen miles to Big Creek together. I put our saddles on two of the mules I had broken to ride and then fished until he was ready to start to the peak. When he came to the hitch rail, he was startled to see our saddles on two mules. He had been hearing tales about how unmanageable those mules had been a couple of years before and just couldn't believe that I was serious about our riding two of them.

Before he would consent to get on his mule, I had first to mount it and ride it around a bit. All the way up to the peak and back to the lake he chuckled about his finally actually riding a mule and wished several dozen times that this or that friend of his could see him now. He would say, "Wait 'til I tell him about this," and he would chuckle some more. It so happened that the mule he was riding worked directly behind mine in the regular string, and up on the ridge where it was wide and grassy, four animals could have walked abreast, but try as he may he could not get that mule up beside mine. It stayed directly behind where it thought it belonged.

After I moved the crew from the lake up to the peak and was packing wire as well as lumber, I would camp alone at the lake at night. There were, of course, grizzly bears in the country, as there always were that near the Whitefish Divide, but when I would go to the meadow at the head of the lake each morning for my stock, I feared the moose more than the grizzlies. Someone was always being treed by a belligerent moose, and every morning I had to pass several that would be feeding in the shallow water near the shore where I had to pass.

I always slept in the trail so that should my stock decide to "pull out" they could not get past without waking me. One night, I was asleep, my feet to the south, and the moon shining from that direction. I was dreaming that some big nameless creature had me down and was holding me. My arms were helpless and I was unable to move. When I gradually awakened, a large porcupine was perched on my chest. When only half awake and looking at the moon over his quilled back, he looked as large as a full-grown grizzly bear. In lurching my body I dumped him off me, and he waddled off into the brush. Had I sat upright or struck at him with my hands when only half awake, I would certainly have gotten my hands and face filled with quills, or even worse, a blow by that thick, powerful tail could have permanently blinded me.

In this especially dry year of 1929, it had gotten so dry that grass was a scarce commodity most places. Because of this, when I was packing the lumber for the two-room cabin being built at Cyclone Park I would usually loose the cinches and allow the stock to graze for two or three hours, as the grass there was luxuriant. One evening I returned late to Big Creek after letting them graze. It was getting rather dusk when I arrived. Jack Lillevig came across the foot-log to the corral to help me unsaddle. One of the meaner mules had a fly bitten area just ahead of the cinch, a favorite spot for them to attack. After unsaddling the animal, I began putting some medication on the sore spot. I always tried to use caution, but with the lessened daylight, I failed to see the toe calk of the mule's hind foot coming at me as it cow-kicked forward. He struck me beside and below the corner of my right eye.

Jack was nearby, and his description was that it sounded "like a board of a peach crate breaking" when the mule's shoe struck me. He took me to Dr. Kell in Columbia Falls for treatment of the wound. I lost no time from work as a result of it, but in the weeks that followed, while it was healing, I had some anxious moments.

By late summer, the men stationed on fire lookouts, and outlying fire guard cabins had begun to tire somewhat of their isolation and craved some sort of entertainment, or just conversation with others. In the evenings, they would get on the huge network of telephones, and anyone who could sing or play a musical instrument would do his act for all listeners. Arkansaw Nelson and Johnny Glover were exceptionally good on harmonicas. (To this day, harmonica music is one of my favorites.) Floyd Rongstead, from the area west of the Whitefish Divide, was an excellent singer and yodeler.

One night, several of us were in the warehouse office listening in on one of those impromptu shows, and an official from the Forest Service regional office who was at the station came in to make a phone call. We had no chance to warn the entertainers, as he went directly to the phone. After

43

trying to get the operator, he turned to us and asked, "Where the hell is all that music coming from?" I told him I had no idea but quickly got on another phone and told the group to layoff for a few minutes, that I'd phone the Forks Cabin when the coast was clear.

Poker for small stakes was another form of amusement out in the camps. On my overnight stays out there I always took some change with me and would get in the game. It seemed that I always won and often have given money I had won back to them so they would have something to play with in future games. On the other hand, when officials from the supervisor's or regional offices came for a few days stay, and there were real poker games for higher stakes, I never had a winning evening. Then I longed for some of the hands I'd had out in the boondocks.

One day when I returned from a routine trip, Jim Bosworth, an assistant supervisor, and Walt Urquhardt were at Big Creek talking with Jack Lillevig. Jack called me over and told me the story. There was a bad fire up near the head of Trail Creek, and no action whatever had been taken on it as no pack string was available and it was far beyond any smokechaser attack. Meanwhile, a fire had broken out up on Moose Creek while Frank Newton was in the vicinity on a routine pack trip with half his string. There were two work teams of horses being used in the area, so packsaddles were sent up, and Frank was packing the four along with his mules, while the remainder of his string was in the pasture at Ford Ranger Station. These men were requesting that I go to Ford and pack to this fire, which had not as yet been named the "Trail Creek Fire." 1929 was to be one of the worst fire years in this century, and the Trail Creek Fire was among the notorious fires. Half a century later, it would still be a topic of conversation, and its effects are still noticeable.

That evening, I trailed my pack string up the North Fork Road to Moran Ranger Station. At four the next morning, I was awakened, got my string ready and after breakfast went on to Ford. Jim Bosworth was at Ford when I arrived, and two twenty-five-man outfits had been delivered, complete with rations. Jim Bosworth was the assistant forest supervisor and a very capable man. He was an expert in forest fire suppression. He was the inventor of the Bosworth map board, a fire location finder, and had also invented a mechanical trencher. He was a Humphrey Bogart type, brusque and impatient. Throughout all of our association where the going was always rough, we were to become very good friends. Bosworth told me that he wanted me to take Frank's extra mules in addition to my string and had sent a fire guard out to get them into the corral. As I was packing the loads for the thirteen pack animals, Harry Pennoyer, the North Fork road crew foreman, and Jimmy Cook, one of his men, arrived. Harry was to go in as a crew foreman. I had seen some sacks of oats in the barn and asked Harry and Jimmy to have some of the men bring a sack to me so I could pack it to take with me, as I could see that my day would be a long one and my stock were sure to be hungry. However, before I could get it packed, Bosworth saw it and said, "No oats this trip, there's too much other stuff that has to go." However, he had more to do than watch me, and in his first absence I got it packed, camouflaged by a roll table top.

From Ford I would be going up Whale Creek to the Semo-Ninko Divide, which was just east of the Mount Thompson–Seton Lookout. The fire was reported to be somewhere in this vicinity. The Ford station fire guard, Paul Lemon, was to accompany me as far as the Semo-Ninko turnoff to help in finding the trail, which from this point was just a "way trail," little more than a foot trail with grades up to 35 percent and many switchbacks. Since my stock was so heavily loaded, and many of the packs extremely bulky, I asked Paul to lead Frank's mules and go ahead of me so that I could keep my eye on all the loads. We had gone no more than two miles when a man came up behind my string and shouted at me to stop.

He then came up past my string and told me that one hundred men had arrived at Ford and had immediately been sent up the trail behind me. This man said that many of the one hundred had eaten no breakfast and that unless they had some food they would be unable to continue on. I quickly decided that the best I could do to furnish them food without cooking would

The ranger dwelling, then newly constructed, and the warehouse at the Glacier View Ranger Station in 1928.

be to send them canned fruit and bread. I knew which packs these items were in, so I quickly unpacked the mules carrying these items, found a couple of burlap sacks in another pack and sent Paul back with the food. I never saw Paul again, and I hope he is not running around somewhere carrying a couple of gunny sacks of fruit and bread, looking for some hungry men. Now leading thirteen pack animals, I found the Semo-Ninko turnoff without difficulty and started negotiating this route, scarcely passable for a jackrabbit. One of Frank's mules, Willie, the smallest and the lightest loaded one in my caravan, was in the caboose (rear), and the trail so crooked and so brushy I would not be able to see him more often than a glimpse about every ten minutes.

Mount Thompson–Seton Lookout was to the west of this divide. The fire had become such a raging holocaust that it threatened not only the lookout station but also the very life of Thomas, the lookout man. He beat a hasty retreat off the peak by the only route open to him. At this point, however, the wind changed, and the spread of the fire was in another direction, so Thomas went back and resumed his duties. Again the wind changed, and Thomas barely escaped this time with his hide unscorched. The building burned minutes after he left it.

After going down the north side of the Semo-Ninko Divide into the Antlie and Trail Creek drainages, I found myself confronted by a solid wall of fire. After sizing up this dangerous situation, I saw what I thought to be a way of getting into a small area of burned-over woods in which the fire had pretty well burned itself out. After studying it for several minutes from the back of my horse (you seem to see better there than from the ground) I decided to stay right where I was for the time being and not go into that dirty, black burn, even though it might be safer in the long run. Within forty-five minutes, the men behind me started arriving. Included among them were Harry Pennoyer, another foreman, and Lawrence Glover, a lad near my age who was a regular forest worker but also a native North Forker, as his parents lived in the upper North Fork. He knew the area very well, having worked two summers in the vicinity.

As more men arrived, there was much indecision as to where to locate the camp. I would not unpack until this verdict was reached, as I wanted to put all their supplies and equipment exactly where they were wanted. Finally, all of those charged with making the decision came to me in a group and asked me what I thought they should do. Included in their group by now was a ranger from another forest who had considerable experience on forest fires. I had already formed my opinion as to what I would do if I were in charge, so

I told them without hesitation, giving my reasons. I said to put the camp in the green timber, where it would be clean and comfortable. Furthermore, the creek water at this point had not run through any of the fire so the danger of dysentery would be lessened. On the other hand, the area I designated was near enough to the small burned out area I had mentioned that they would always have an escape route. They agreed fully, and it was done as I suggested. The visiting ranger later thanked me and complimented me on my judgment. I had too many other things on my mind to waste time at feeling flattered that they would ask a twenty-year-old. Incidentally, the escape route was used temporarily just a few days later.

I quickly dropped the packs from the stock, and as soon as the most urgently needed items were unpacked I opened the 100-pound sack of smuggled oats and fed the stock. By now it was dusk, and since my day had started at four that morning, I began looking for a place to graze them. As I was doing this, a few men came into the camp from the Trail Creek side. One of them, another ranger, handed me a letter from Jim Bosworth. It was in a sealed envelope and was an order for me to come to the Tom Peterson homestead on Trail Creek, where a base camp had been set up. From what the ranger who had brought the letter had told me about their last mile before reaching camp, I could see that it would not be easy taking fourteen head of stock through that mile of fire at night. I finally prevailed upon those in charge to send Lawrence Glover to guide me through that part. He knew the area well, whereas I had never been over it.

At the Tom Peterson place where the base camp had been set up, I found that horse feed had been delivered and a night cook was on duty at the kitchen. When I had taken care of the feeding of my stock and was ready for a bedtime snack, I noted that this day's work had been just forty minutes short of twenty-four hours. I was up again two hours later, and that day made two trips to the fire in an effort to catch up with the tremendous amount of freight to be taken in. More men were coming in, and the supplies were now coming directly from the region warehouse in Missoula.

The second morning at Trail Creek, sleeping with my ear close to the ground, I was awakened by the sound of trucks approaching. At first I thought the trucks to be within a half mile, but as time passed I realized that they had been at least four miles away, on the main North Fork Road, when I had first heard them. When they arrived, there were more groceries, tools and camp equipment, such as Kimmel stoves, tent flies, etc. In addition to the supplies, nearly one hundred more men came in that morning. More trucks arrived as I finished the feeding of my stock, and many of the hobo type firefighters who had come in on them soon were making pests of themselves by approaching the tied-up stock, causing the wilder ones to pull back on their halters.

After I had got them cleared out, I started saddling and soon noticed that one man had remained and was intently watching me as I worked. He was a large Mexican fellow, wearing well-fitting though worn Levi's and a large Stetson hat. When I looked his way, he approached me and asked if he might help me saddle up. I gave him a few pointers on how I wanted the job done and showed him the animal that the top saddle in the stack belonged on. I could tell by the way he approached the animal and put the pads and saddle on that he had done this thing many times before. He did, however, make a mistake that I had seen too many packers and horsemen make, and a thing I am fussy about—that was not to put the pads far enough forward. They work back fifty times more often than they ever work forward, so I showed him how far forward to put them. He was never to make this mistake again, nor did I ever have to show him twice the things I wanted done.

After he had helped me load the string, he told me that he greatly enjoyed helping me with the saddling and packing and asked me if there might be a chance that he could remain in camp and fix a better place to feed and tie up the stock. I had much appreciated his help, as he did everything well yet would do it exactly as I wanted it done. Jim Bosworth argued and protested when I asked that this man, Taylor Valarde, be allowed to remain in camp as my helper. I finally got a little bit aggravated and pointed out to him how much help cooks, foremen and timekeepers had, and I even alluded to many of his own duties he delegated to others. He had no good argument for the latter, so Taylor was allowed to remain in camp. Valarde had worked with stock all his life so had many good ideas for improvements during the day while I was gone, and when I was in camp he never left my side.

The morning of the fourth day, two men rode into camp from the north. Jim Bosworth told me that one was a Forest Warden from British Columbia who had come to check on the chances of the fire invading his domain. Before I was packed they rode off toward Frozen Lake. The wound on my upper right cheekbone near my eye where I had been kicked had been causing a great deal of pain, and I remember that this morning I examined it, looking in the side mirror of a truck. It had healed very slowly, perhaps because of improper dressing and the fact that at night I would scrape the dressing off as I thrashed around in my sleep. There was a considerable amount of pus in the wound, and besides the constant pain, I was greatly worried by the twitching of the involuntary muscles surrounding it. It even occurred to me that I might lose my eye.

On this fifth day, I made only one trip, and although I started later than usual, I was back in camp by mid-afternoon. I was delighted to see that Frank Newton had arrived a short time before. We compared notes on what each of us had been doing and cargoed some loads for the next day's trip. Of course, Taylor Valarde was on hand as always to lend a hand. That night we bedded down under the overhang of Peterson's barn, where I had been bunking. I was just about asleep when a man came up and knelt beside me, putting a hand on my shoulder asking, "Where is Frank Newton sleeping?"

I told him that Frank was sleeping beside me, whereupon he hopped over me and started talking with Frank. I paid no attention to what he was saying until I heard him ask Frank, "Where's that kid that packs for Lillevig?"

When Frank told him that it was the guy that he had been talking with first, he took off on the run and soon was back with an Imperial quart of Canadian whisky. A drink of whisky was about the last thing I would have asked for about then, but I made a show of drinking and thanked him. The next morning, the Canadian warden left for home, but this man, Charlie Wise, remained with us. Charlie was a transplanted easterner who was to become a sort of legend in the North Fork. A story is told of his having snowshoed all the way out of the upper North Fork carrying his little girl, who had swallowed a safety pin. Tragically, he lost both her and his wife later in a flu epidemic.

The second morning that Frank was there, we had loaded and were less than a mile up the trail when we met a half dozen men hurrying down the trail, waving their arms and shouting. When they got to us, we were told that the camp had burned in a sudden blowup of the fire and that six men had died in the kitchen. They said that others might have also perished, but they were sure of those six. We turned back and I located Walter Urquhardt to listen to their story. He soon got hold of Bosworth, and the decision was made for Frank and me to each take three mules to the camp to pack out the bodies. Urquhardt would go in with us. As we unpacked we decided which mules we would take for this grisly task, and we were ready to start when a man came trotting into the camp and asked if we had seen six wild men with a wild story about the camp burning. He then assured us that the camp had not burned, although there had been a flare-up and they had been obliged to retreat into the burned over spot that I had shown them at the beginning to be a good escape route.

About this time, three more pack strings had been ordered and had finally arrived at the base camp. That evening when Frank and I arrived back at camp, Roland Tibbets, Bill Grant and Vern Drake were there with their horse strings and their sawbuck saddles. Now that Frank Newton and the three private strings were on the job, the camp well stocked and with more fires starting farther south, my orders were to return to Big Creek, now called the Glacier View Ranger Station.

It had been a workout for me those past several days, working alone packing thirteen head and constantly hounded by Jim Bosworth to load heavier. Taylor Valarde had been a lot of help but totally inexperienced in packing except for what he could learn from me in my haste.

On the morning of August 21, 1929, from this base camp three and a half miles south of the British Columbia border and an equal distance west of the North Fork River, I headed south. I had no regrets to be leaving this camp, although I knew the workload of merely supplying a camp once it has been established is much lighter. Furthermore, every mile of trail I had been leading that thirteen-head string was a gauntlet of yellow jacket nests. My animals and I were collecting dozens of stings causing innumerable wrecks. In dry years like 1929, yellow jackets are especially prevalent, it seems.

By the time I reached the North Fork Road, I could see a large cloud of smoke a great distance to the south. The cloud rapidly got larger and darker. Within a couple of hours it had taken on a really ominous appearance, with a huge cloud of steam showing above the smoke. Even at that distance I could see huge flames above the fire rise several hundred feet in the air. This was the gas of the green timber being consumed. At times when I would stop I would imagine that I could actually hear it roar. I made forty-five-minute stops at Ford Ranger Station and at Moran to rest, feed and water my stock.

All during the forenoon I had overtaken men hurrying down the road. They were deserters from the fire. Many had been conscripted from the streets of nearby towns or from freight trains. They paid little attention to me as I passed them except that occasionally one of them would shout to ask for a ride on one of my animals. When they would hear a truck or automobile coming, they would scurry behind brush or trees at the roadside. They were terrified of being sent back to the fire.

I arrived at Big Creek about 4:00 or 4:30 that afternoon, having traveled about thirty-five miles with my empty string. Jack Lillevig was at the station. He had driven south in the afternoon, past the National Forest Boundary, to get what information he could on the fire's progress. At the boundary camp he told John Sutherland, stationed there to check cars coming into the forest, to tear down his tents and pack up everything, as he was sending a truck to pick up everything. In ten minutes he was back and told Sutherland to grab what he could and get in the car. The fire was almost upon them. They told me that they were sure the camp had burned fifteen minutes after they left it.

This was the Half Moon Fire, the most notorious of the 1929 fires. It would burn 103,400 acres, 39,000 within Glacier, and it destroyed several small towns such as Coram and Apgar. Calder's store at Lake Five burned. In an article published in the November 1929 issue of the University of Montana *Frontier Magazine*, Mr. Grisbourne of the U.S. Forest Service regional office in Missoula wrote, "Homes, ranches, and small saw mills were reduced to heaps of ashes, small patches of fused china and glassware, and twisted metal bedsteads. Drive shafts of mills twisted, and saws cracked. Families lost all that they had struggled throughout their lives to acquire."

[Editor's note: The Half Moon Fire was the worst fire to strike Glacier in the author's lifetime. In recorded history to date, the 1929 devastation within the Park is exceeded only by several fires in 2003 that consumed 139,000 acres in Glacier. In 1910, a huge forest fire complex, the worst in American history, reached Glacier. Culminating in what was called the "Big Blowup," the 1910 fires were mainly concentrated in the Idaho panhandle, but flames spread across much of northwestern Montana, destroying about 3 million acres.]

When I started working in Glacier Park a few years later, many people who were there at the time of the 1929 fire gave me their accounts of their experiences. Up to that time the two-mile drive, or walk, between Belton (later West Glacier) and Apgar had been one of unparalleled beauty. Huge Western Red Cedar trees closely bordered the narrow road. Today the road, the main entrance to Glacier National Park, is bounded by a dense forest of short jack pine.

Gus Aubert, Ida Goos, Ed Swetman, Hub Chatterton, Ace Powell Sr., Heinie and Cora Hutchens, Leona Harrington, Art Lewis and Otis Alderson were all in the Belton and Apgar area when the 1929 fire struck. Ida Goos had her fine home in Apgar burned but replaced it soon after.

Nancy Russell, the wife of the great Montana artist Charles M. Russell, who had been living at their place that had been Russell's summer studio at Apgar on the southern end of Lake McDonald, gave me her account. Their home, where they entertained in summer many prominent guests before his death in 1926, was a little way around the lake to the left from the outlet. It was spared and stands today, as does the studio cabin. Mary Roberts Rinehart, Irvin S. Cobb, Howard Eaton, Judge Bollinger (one of

The billowing clouds of smoke from the Half Moon Fire of 1929 as it reaches the southwestern edge of Glacier National Park. *National Park Service photo.*

Russell's hunting chums) and Powder River Jack and Kitty were some of the famous guests that Russell invited to his summer home. I remember seeing Russell at Apgar in 1923 when he had just come back from watching Jack Dempsey defend his heavyweight title against Tommy Gibbons in the ring in Shelby, Montana. In my mind, I can still picture him in his gray suit, the crown of his hat blown up and his red sash around his waist. He liked to talk.

George Slack sent up a fire pump, and Bill Bose was credited saving several homes with his pump. That summer I packed dozens of these marine fire pumps to fire camps and many times had to show the men operating

them how to start and operate them. During the next forty years, there was practically no change in their style and operation.

Belton is situated about a mile south of Apgar and Lake McDonald beside the Middle Fork of the Flathead River on US Highway 2 and the main line of what was then the Great Northern Railway. The Headquarters of Glacier National Park are across the river. At the Headquarters of the Park there was much confusion and difference of opinion as to what to do. There were many marine pumps on hand, and they were placed along the river. A swath that is now a street in the residential area was cut for a fire break. All structures were saved. The swath today continues on up the hill toward the water reservoir.

*Right*: Charles M. Russell, the famous Montana artist, maintained a home and studio in Apgar at the foot of Lake McDonald. The 1929 fire came close to destroying these, but they survived. *Photographer unknown, public domain.*

*Below*: In this watercolor, Charles M. Russell depicted two deer at the edge of Lake McDonald in front of his Apgar studio. Deer are still often seen in exactly this location. *Charles M. Russell, public domain.*

The author (*right*) and his son, W.P. Yenne (*left*), with a friend on top of Apgar Mountain in August 1960. Lake McDonald can be seen below, with the mountains of the Lewis Range at the head of the lake. The area around the foot of the lake was then still recovering from the fires of 1929. The rolling hills on the left would burn again in 2003.

The heat was so intense in much of the fire's path that to this day there has been no reforestation. The fire burned less than a mile up the east side of Lake McDonald, along which the Going-to-the-Sun Road runs.

Lake McDonald is named after Duncan McDonald of the Flathead Indian tribe. Sometime along about the middle of the nineteenth century, he and his party were returning from a skirmish with the Blackfeet to the east, and he had carved his name on a tree on its shore. In the years to come, people would see that name on the tree and started calling the lake by that name.

McDonald was born in 1849 at Fort Connah near Dixon. His father, Angus McDonald, had built the fort two years before. Angus was a native of Scotland, and his wife, Duncan's mother, was a Nez Perce Indian woman.

When I arrived back at the Big Creek Ranger Station on the evening of August 21, I made sure that my stock were well cared for and given every attention I could give them. I cleaned their backs, inspected their feet, reset some shoes and fed them well. There was little to do at the ranger station but wait until the fire had slowed down somewhat and then plan an attack along its flank to keep it from widening. We made a couple of

The author not infrequently crossed paths with Charles M. Russell at the Lake McDonald Hotel on the east shore of the lake ten miles from Apgar. Built in 1913 by John Lewis, it was originally known as the Lewis Glacier Hotel. It was acquired by the Great Northern Railway in 1935 and renamed Lake McDonald Lodge in 1957. *W.P. Yenne.*

The interior of the Lake McDonald Hotel as it appeared around the time that Russell knew it. The animal heads, part of John Lewis's own collection, are still part of the hotel's décor.

reconnaissance trips down the road toward its northern perimeter, keeping a sharp lookout for flare-ups.

On the second of these scouting missions, it was decided that in an hour or so it might be possible for a couple of men to get through on the road in an attempt to establish communication by splicing the telephone line. The road itself of course was completely blocked by fallen timber. John Sutherland, the man who had manned the entrance camp, and I were chosen to make the attempt. At about 8:30 that evening, we set out equipped with head flashlights, a portable telephone, tree climbers, linemen's tools such as Klein pliers, connectors, comealongs, etc., and a supply of number nine galvanized wire.

The fire had been so fiercely hot that it had completely consumed everything easily burnable such as brush, branches and even the smaller trees. Larger trees were still afire, giving us some additional light at times. We had to be on the lookout for live coals, especially in depressions, and had many close calls from falling trees.

In many places, we were obliged to climb over labyrinths of newly fallen logs that were still burning. At times our task would appear utterly hopeless in the darkness. Neither of us gave a thought to giving up—we just knew that we'd make it somehow.

Both John and I had been involved in boxing as youths, and we had boxed with each other dozens of times, being about the same size. In corresponding with John many years later, he would refer to me as his "boxing adversary." John Sutherland later became a movie producer, working for 20th Century Fox and for Disney Productions as a writer and production executive. He was coauthor of the original story of *Flight Command*, which starred Robert Taylor, Walter Pidgeon and Ruth Hussey. During World War II, he was a production supervisor and the writer of 108 reels of training films for the U.S. Army and Navy. Since World War II, his own production house has become widely known as John Sutherland Productions.

The number nine galvanized wire, a little more than one-eighth inch in diameter, had gotten so hot that it would stretch to one-thirty-second of an inch diameter or less and then would break. Where we had to splice it, which was sometimes every few yards, the ends had long tapers that were almost needle sharp where they had broken. Every twenty minutes or so, we would hook up our little test phone and call back to Big Creek, where Helmer Jensen, the commissary clerk, was on duty. If we couldn't get Helmer, then we'd have to go back and check for a break we had missed. He in turn kept trying to call the operator in Columbia Falls. Our shins were rubbed raw from climbing over hot logs. Our feet were burned from stepping in holes full of coals. Our hands were raw from all the pulling and splicing there in the dark. The light from the head flashlights seemed to be always in the wrong place, even though we had learned they were more effective around the neck than on the head.

About three o'clock in the morning we were so tired we were practically rolling over logs rather than stepping or crawling over them. Still, Helmer would tell us that he hadn't gotten through to Columbia Falls. Finally, as it was getting daylight enough that we could see each other without lights, we listened in as Helmer made another try and heard the voice of Lottie Lenon, the Columbia Falls operator, loud and clear as she answered, "Columbia." I'll never forget how that one word sounded there in the semi-darkness. We had done it! Sutherland and I grinned and shook hands with each other, our teeth gleaming white through our black faces, "our two black hands gripping in the dawn," as Keats might have said.

After we got back to Big Creek that morning and had some breakfast and a few hours' sleep, I was sent on a scouting mission along the north edge of the burned area west of the North Fork Road. I worked as a fire scout for two more days, and then another urgent call came from the upper district. Two fires that had gone undetected for several days because lookouts had not been able to see their smoke in the smoke-laden air were discovered to have grown to major proportions.

Again I headed north with my pack string, headed for Ford Station, where I was to receive orders as to which drainage I would pack from and so forth. Upon reaching Ford Station, which was completely deserted and fully locked, I loosed the cinches of all my saddles and fed the stock some grain. I went to the ranger station/cook house, where I managed to get a window open and crawl through. As I was starting to look for something I could eat, the phone started to ring. I knew the Ford Station ring, so I answered. It was Jim Bosworth calling, and the call was for me.

It seemed that the two fires I had been sent to pack to had now been scouted and were spreading so rapidly that any attempt to put camps on them or flank them would be dangerous, even foolhardy. Instead, I was to return to Moran Ranger Station, where there were other fires for which a plan of attack was being made.

Back at Moran there was much delay in getting the material I was to pack to the first of the fires, and only a part of the crew to be sent in were on hand. When everything was finally gotten together, and I had packed my stringload, it was nearly dark. When I started for the fire, all of the men, including the overhead, fell in behind me. Although the trail was new to me, I was the guide there in the darkness. I had a head flashlight slung around my neck, my loads perfectly balanced and Sam, my saddle horse, was as dependable as the passing of time. When we came to the place where we were to leave the trail, there was a leaf from Thayer's notebook with some information written on it under the heading of "Farina Kid." As usual, it was signed "Thayer."

There were not nearly enough head flashlights for the crew, and going in like this in the dark, morale was at a low ebb. Even the overhead, strangers even to Montana, were in low spirits. I remember particularly that first night a Forest Officer from Arizona who had been flown in to help fight our fires. I was able to be of great assistance to him that night in getting organized at the scene of the fire camp. I learned later that I had boosted his morale greatly as well. I wish that I had made a note of his name so that I could write it here because we became very close friends in the next weeks, and he repaid those favors many times over when the going was rough for me.

As on the first night, I had to keep a sharp lookout for leaves from Thayer's notebook. I recall feeling ashamed a few times when I would temporarily lose the route, and the crews behind me would be obliged to wait for me to get back on track. As I mentioned, there were times when Sam found it before me, causing me to believe he could read what those yellow notebook pages meant. When we arrived at the Cyclone Lake camp on the night run, there were loons out on the lake. I can still hear their mournful laugh.

In the next two and a half weeks, night packing became the rule for me. I would get back to the base about daylight or shortly after, have something to eat after caring for my stock, then I'd try to get some sleep. There was noise, heat, flies crawling over my face and usually an uncomfortable bed to interfere with complete rest.

Some other packers with short horse strings had been hired to help me in servicing the camps once I had them established. While they packed in the daytime, I couldn't seem to shake that nocturnal run. Each evening at dusk a truck or two would roll in from the Missoula warehouse with critically needed supplies, and since my stock and I had "rested" during the day, I was again elected to take it to its designated camp. I'm not sure that winning all those elections was good or bad, but I never lost one.

I had not been unhappy to leave the Trail Creek Fire and the camp at Torn Peterson's, but now I longed to be back there where, in talking with Frank Newton, I learned that they were enjoying practically "banker's hours," routinely servicing the camps I had packed in while there. Frank told me that for a time they had put Taylor Valarde packing his string, and

Results of a "wildfire hurricane" in a heavy stand of white pine on the Little North Fork of St. Joe River in Idaho, which occurred during the great firestorm of 1910. Reaching as far as Glacier, this was a precursor to the 1929 Half Moon Fire, which created similar devastation. The author witnessed the results of 1910 when he worked in the St. Joe Country in the late 1920s. *Library of Congress.*

he had been made a sort of "head packer." I remember that I asked Frank whether he wore a suit and necktie in that new, lofty position.

In the daytime, after I had had my "rest," I would look about for some sort of diversion. Les Jones, the head cook, and Clark Hamor, commissary clerk, were good company, and we had many good talkfests. One day, in an incident that we still laugh about, Clark and I discovered that there was a large weasel in the grocery room of the warehouse and at once set about to capture him. When he was finally cornered, I was the one wearing gloves, so I caught him. He bit through the thick leather of the glove and deeply into my finger.

A North Fork rancher named Fletcher "Hooly" Stein had a homestead adjoining the Moran Ranger Station on the south. He had a herd of Hereford cattle that every afternoon would come to the ranger station yard to get in the shade of the buildings. If the barn door was left open, they would go into the barn to escape the flies. As soon as I saw these cattle in the barn, I started figuring out a way to practice steer riding on them. It was not possible to get the barn door open once you were aboard one of them, so I had to have some help. There was a tall, lean young fellow of my own age, with a long, German-sounding name working there as a sort of flunkey, or roustabout helping the cooks.

He and I struck up a friendship, and as I was in need of a helper or "chute tender," I started talking steer riding to him. He was from back east somewhere and had never heard of such a thing, but with my sales talk he could see the possibilities of some fun. In order not to lose the rope, I would take a piece of three-eighths-inch rope, long enough to reach around the critter's girth when doubled. Once the doubled rope was around him, I'd run the two ends through the doubled loop and grasp the four ropes with one hand. With the free hand I would pull it as tight as possible and then hold the tension with my hand.

At the end of the ride the rope would fall off before he had gone far. Once I was ready, my chute tender would open the barn door, and we were on our way. As anticipated, my helper soon wanted to give it a try, so I coached him in the finer points of steer riding. I'm sure that he had never even ridden a gentle horse in his life, but after being tossed sky high a couple of times he seemed to develop a natural aptitude for it. After a couple of successful rides, he was as enthusiastic as I was. This went on for several days, but as we rode more of these cattle, they became so wary that we could not get them into the ranger station yard.

One day I had helped Dewey Parrish, one of the other packers, load his horse string for a trip to one of the camps. His string was short and could not take all the freight that was supposed to go, so I put a packsaddle on a big, young work horse named Bill. Bill belonged to the Forest Service but had been running loose in Hooly Stein's pasture. He had been somewhat hard to saddle and pack but was well halter broken, so I assumed that since he was a broken draft animal, he would soon quiet down and would be a good pack horse. He weighed well over 1,500 pounds, so I had put a fairly heavy load on him. I tied him in the caboose end of Dewey's string and sent them on their way. The trailhead was not far from the station, and I watched Dewey ride out of sight. Bill had done a lot of dancing and prancing with his load but led well and had made no attempt to buck.

I had been careful to select goods for his load that didn't rattle. Five minutes later, Bill came charging into the ranger station yard minus his packs and with both sling ropes dragging. I caught him, tied him up and then trotted out to see how Dewey had weathered the storm. Dewey was okay; he had tied up his string and was coming back to see about Bill. I told him to go on, that I would pick up the scattered goods. Through all this I had noticed that Bill, in spite of his bulk, had the light-footed action of a 1,000-pound roping horse. In thinking about it he somehow reminded me of the Big Four, the bay horses in Mike Reed's bucking string that I had encountered at rodeos, the famous Fearsome Foursome that had bucked off so many of the top riders of North America.

Having the rodeo fever as I had, I was determined to see just how hard he could buck. There was no one around that I felt I could depend on to haze for me if I tried him, so with the help of Harold Cusick, the alternate, I loaded two stout wooden boxes on him, first putting a handful of small rocks in each for noise. When turned loose in the fenced enclosure, he fully lived up to my expectations of him as a bucking horse. I firmly believed then, and still do, that if he could have been put in a major bucking string at that time he would have proven to be as good a saddle bronc as the best of them.

The next summer, when we were somewhat short of saddle animals, Jack Lilliveg suggested to me that we get him to use as an extra saddle horse. I told Jack that I didn't think either of us was man enough to ride him. Jack swore that he had used him the winter before as half of a driving team and that he had become gentle. He kept insisting, so one day we went up to Hooly's pasture and managed to catch him with the help of a nosebag of oats. I put my Hamley Association saddle on him, but it was a bit of a fight. I told the fellows that if I got bucked off I didn't want him running around loose with my saddle, so I thought I'd try him in the large log corral at Hooly's barn.

By the time we had led him the quarter mile to the corral, he had become so quiet that I began to think that maybe he wouldn't buck after all. There were some fishermen there and I thought it might be nice to treat them to a good bronc ride, so I put my spurs high in his shoulders and told the fellows to turn him loose. In all my rodeo riding I have never been bucked off as cleanly as he unloaded me that day. In his fifth jump he seemed to get me high in the air, then just literally jerked the saddle out from under me. I had a good landing without any jarring, and as I landed I could see the light-colored side of his underbelly directly above me. I borrowed a snaffle bit from Hooly, which I fastened to his halter, and succeeded in riding him the second time. I rode him more than half the way to Big Creek. I rode him a few times after that, but he continued to be hard to mount and was always so nervous and skittish that I didn't want to risk trying to lead a string of mules off him. I used him occasionally as a supplement to my pack string, where he worked fine in the caboose because he led so well, and in that position he had nothing behind him to spook him.

At Big Creek one evening the following year, around supper time, two Canadian border patrolmen came to the cookhouse where we were eating and told us that there had been an automobile wreck at Deep Creek a mile to the south. Shorty Waters, in his Essex touring car, had failed to make the curve on the north side of the creek. In the auto were three other passengers: Hooly Stein and two elderly gents, a Mr. Price and a Mr. Jorden, the latter having rolled and tumbled nearly two hundred feet to the streambed. Shorty sustained broken ribs, one of which punctured a lung, causing an air bubble up by his shoulder. Hooly received a compound fracture of a shin bone. By the time we got there, he had crawled all the way up to the road and had removed the sock from his injured leg and hung it on a bush, where it hung for weeks afterward. One of the other men was killed outright; the other died on the way to the hospital in Kalispell.

At about the same time Bill bucked off Dewey's load, there was a blowup of the existent fires, caused by high winds, followed by more lightning. More men were sent, and they were followed by more materials to pack. There were not enough pack stock to handle the workload, and as the Flathead Valley had been drained of pack stock, a call was made to the Park Service in Glacier. They also had their fires and all their stock was in use, so our order was passed on to the Park's horse concessionaire, Noffsinger's Bar-X-Six. The order had been for thirty-six pack animals, the thought being that this would be four nine-head strings. The Bar-X-Six, however, were still using the old sawbuck saddles and the three-quarter diamond hitch, with only five pack animals to a string. Therefore, they had their seven best packers from the various parts of the Park converge at Lake McDonald. From there they trailed up the road on the Park side of the North Fork River to Polebridge and then from there to Moran Ranger Station.

It was a sight to remember, to see seven well-dressed cowboys, wearing long yellow slickers, riding into the ranger station yard in the rain driving thirty-five loose pack horses. Glacier Park was a roistering, fun-loving place for the dude wranglers in those days, and among this group were some very good poker players. Some of the top Forest Service officials were staying the night at Moran, and they also were good at the game, so a very notable game went on all that first night at Moran Station.

Meanwhile, out in the fire camps the men had to eat, rain or shine, and the pumps needed gasoline. The private horse strings had all been out on trips that

Charles M. Russell drew this sketch of a Bar-X-Six guide and his party on a letter that he wrote to Guy Wendrick of the TS Ranch in Alberta in November 1921. *Charles M. Russell, public domain.*

day, and the Bar-X-Six horses of course were considered too legweary to make a trip. Nevertheless, the never-ending stream of trucks from Missoula arrived at dusk, so I loaded up and headed out as usual into the dark, rainy night. It rained all that night, but not nearly as hard as the honchos (officials) thought. The next morning, they decided that the thirty-five head of Bar-X-Six pack stock were far too many, now that the fall rains had set in, so decided to send five of the seven packers back to the Park. The two that were to stay would increase the size of their strings to six head. Their stock had made a lot of miles the day they arrived, so they were given a day to rest before starting back.

When I got back to Moran that morning, the honchos and the Bar-X-Six cowboys were getting up after their nocturnal game of chance and were making the decisions just mentioned. Vern Blanchard was the regular packer for Sun Camp in the Park, and Albert Vaile was a good packer, so they were the ones who stayed on to help me with the packing. The officials left before noon, probably, I thought, to go somewhere and get some more sleep.

In visiting with the cowboys, the talk turned to rodeo and bronc riding, as the Bar-X-Six owned nearly 1,500 head of horses, and being range raised, there was bound to be many that would test their riders every morning. I learned from some of them that one of the Bar-X-Six packers, Frank Ramberg, was considered one of the best riders working for the saddle horse company. Talk then turned to some of the pack horses they had brought and the fact that many were pack horses because they could not be broken from bucking. I showed them the fenced enclosure where I had let big Bill buck with the equipment boxes, and soon six of the spoiled horses from their remuda were roped. Three of us—Ramberg, myself and one of the others—rode two of those pack horses each. From the first mention to me of Ramberg's prowess as a bronc rider, my thought was to get him on Bill. I made no mention of our past experience with him, only told them that he was a work horse and that I thought he might buck. Try as I might, I could not talk Ramberg or any of the others into getting on him.

Grizzly bears were always present around camps, and I always saw one or more in making trips into the backcountry, especially the Whitefish Divide region. They soon began showing up at all the fire camps because of the great amount of garbage that was thrown into the pits. One morning, shortly after the five Bar-X-Six cowboys had gone back to the Park, I was returning to the Moran Ranger Station yard at daylight and heard gunshots coming from the small cookhouse. A very large grizzly had torn some boards from a corner of the cookhouse and was enlarging the hole when Les Jones, the head cook who was sleeping in the room, killed him with his new .30-06 rifle.

The bear that Les killed was among the half dozen largest I have ever seen and probably the largest I had seen up to that time. Many of the old-time North Forkers, and others who heard of the incident, came to have a look at the bear, and most estimated his weight in the 900-pound range. I have wished since that we had figured out a way to have weighed him on the platform Fairbanks scales in the warehouse.

This would be a good place to put in a good word about the Forest Service cooks. I never saw a poor one, and what they could do with those plain, staple Forest Service groceries was nothing short of amazing. Earlier I mentioned Madison Turner as one of the North Fork truck drivers and Charlie Hollingworth as the cook at the base camp at Tom Peterson's. In 1974, I had lunch with Madison Turner and his wife at a restaurant in San Francisco. It was the first I had seen him since the fall of 1930. When we started to reminisce, the first name he mentioned was that of Charlie Hollingworth. Another famous cook we remembered was Charlie Conn. He could act more fierce than any tiger but had a heart of gold. We used to say that if he was mad when he washed his dishtowels, they were perfectly dry when he put them on the line.

At Big Creek we had a former railroad dining car cook, and he was a good one. He never failed to have freshly baked rolls for the crew's supper every night. One evening, shortly after he came to Big Creek, I came in from a trip and arrived at the barn and corral just as the supper gong sounded. I unsaddled and fed my stock and then crossed the foot-log and washed. I was met at the cookhouse door by a very big, and very angry, cook. He said, "I saw you come in just as I rang for supper, but no, you wait until everyone else is through eating, then expect me to feed you."

I explained to him that my stock always ate first, no matter what, and if he did not want to feed me I knew where the can openers and groceries were kept in the warehouse. We got along just fine after that.

Some of the fire camps were not moved out until October, and I recall packing some of them when there were four inches of snow on the ground. Back at Big Creek there were plans to continue the interrupted trail construction.

I packed two large camps out to far corners of the district, had finished cargoing a third and was ready to go out the following day when word came from the regional office to immediately suspend all new work and spending. When I went out to pack in one of the camps I had already packed out, there was no one at the camp. The crew had been laid off, and it was deserted. It was October 1929, and back east on Wall Street the stock market had just crashed. The nation had just fallen into its deepest depression.

It was a two-day trip, and I was spending the night there. At the time I was going to bed, three grizzlies came to the camp. There were signs that they had been there the previous night. One of them, a medium-sized one, was very bold and in a bad mood. He would approach very close to where I was, and no amount of brandishing a mattock handle or throwing rocks would make him retreat more than a few paces. At times that grizzly got so close that I had thoughts of climbing a tree. All three were circling about within one hundred feet of the camp, with this one sometimes coming to within twenty feet of me. I never let go of the mattock handle or an axe. Finally, about eleven o'clock my stock came into camp. It was moose country where they had been grazing, and I think they had been spooked by a belligerent moose. This was timely for me, as I then caught all of them and tied them in a level glade one hundred yards below the camp and made my bed among them.

I had been riding Jack Lilliveg's horse, Murphy, occasionally during the summer when Jack had no chance to use him. Murphy had been an exhibition bucking horse when owned by the Bar-X-Six; his name then was "Kalispell." He had eventually quit bucking, and Gene Sullivan had purchased him and renamed him. Later, he sold him to Jack. When I took the stock to Columbia Falls, where I was to meet the South and Middle Fork packers that fall, I was alone on the stock drive. In the twenty-one miles from Big Creek to Columbia

Blackfeet National Forest ranger C.J. "Jack" Lillevig and his horse Murphy.

Falls, I usually changed horses at least once. At times when the herd would decide to travel fast, I would get ahead of them to hold back the faster ones. When they tended to lag, I would ride behind them. On this trip, I had roped Murphy near Fool Hen Hill and put my saddle on him, as my other mount had grown legweary from having to pass the herd many times.

At the road to the old Teakettle Ranger Station, the upper district bell mare that was in the lead decided to turn in on that road. Not wishing for the delay and confusion of having them all go into the old station, I took a shortcut through the freshly burned timber to head her off. Murphy was hurdling fallen timber like a steeplechaser when, as he jumped over one of them, he landed in a snarl of old telephone wire. In the next few seconds he showed me that he had not completely forgotten how to buck. Luckily for me, on the first jump my right hand landed squarely on the saddle horn, or I'd probably have ended up in the ashes with some number nine wire around my neck. As he bucked, he continued forward so that I headed the stock successfully.

Both Murphy and Sam wintered at my parents' farm that winter.

The cover of the mimeographed newsletter announcing the 1930 Northern Region Packer's Contest. The illustrations are by Viggo Christensen, whose work appears in many Forest Service publications from this era.

## Chapter 4

# THE YEAR 1930 AND THE NORTHERN REGION PACKERS' CONTEST

During the summer of 1930, my brother Tom's best friend, Bill Reimer, was the lookout man on Nasukoin Mountain in the North Fork's upper district. At an elevation of 8,095 feet, it was the highest point in the Blackfeet National Forest. Some sheep men had a grazing permit in the forest and were at that time grazing them on Shorty Creek below Nasukoin. They were laundering their bedding and, not wishing to alarm the lookouts with a smoke in the daytime, were doing it at night, when the smoke would not be seen. One lookout, however, saw the blaze and so was ordered to go to the fire.

When he reached the valley floor after descending Nasukoin, he leaned his back against a tree to ease the weight of the smokechaser pack for a moment. He then became aware that some sort of animal was approaching him in the darkness. He quickly shed his pack and started to beat a hasty retreat. In the darkness, he tripped over a root and fell to the ground. The animal, a large grizzly bear, was on him instantly. He lay on his back, and for a short time he was able to keep it at bay by kicking it with his calked boots. Suddenly, the grizzly seized one of his feet in its mouth and lifted Bill into the air. Although he is of average height, his shoulders barely touched the ground as the bear shook and twisted at his leg, dislocating his hip.

As this was taking place, he unfastened his holster strap and got out his .38-caliber revolver. He fired three shots low into the bear's body, afraid to shoot higher at the risk of hitting his foot. With each bullet the bear became more fierce and shook all the harder. Finally, in desperation, he decided to try for a more vital spot, hitting his foot or no. Accordingly, he aimed toward the top part of the bear and fired again. This produced the desired results, as the bear let go of his foot and ambled off into the darkness.

Bill was drenched with blood from the bear's earlier wounds, and his damaged hip joint prevented his walking. He practically crawled the distance back to his lookout post. After resting a few moments, he rang Ford Station on the telephone. Phil Harding, the cook, was sleeping in the room where the phone was and in an instant was answering it. Bill identified himself and started to tell of his experience and his plight, but at this point he passed out. Phil reported this to Bert Bealey at Moran at once, and then he and Taylor Valarde, the packer who had been my helper the summer before, went to Nasukoin Lookout, leading a spare saddle animal. Harding was the first to enter the cabin. He was so horrified at the sight before him that he took a step backward, bumping into Valarde behind him. Bill was covered with bear's blood from his hair to his feet and was lying in his bunk, only partly conscious.

It was some weeks before his hip was in condition for him to walk normally, and it bothered him for years to come. He had occasional nightmares and would wake up screaming as his dreams re-created the horrible episode.

That fall, six of us—including Bill; my brother, Tom; and Harry Jessup—were on a ten-day elk hunting trip in the Pentagon Cabin area on Spotted Bear River. Bill's hip was causing him some pain, but he was able to ride a horse without difficulty as he and Tom trailed our stock both ways over the mountains between Spotted Bear and Echo Ranger Station.

Our first camp was at the big falls of the Spotted Bear River below Pentagon Cabin. On the second day, Tom wounded a bull elk three miles above the river and succeeded in driving it to within two hundred yards of the river and trail, where he killed it. A couple of days later, we moved on to Limestone. On the day of the move, we heard an elk bugling across the river near Limestone in the area closed to hunting. Hank Marken answered the bugling and succeeded in luring a large bull across the river, where he shot him as he stepped out of the water. The 1930 season had been another very busy one for me. There were a large number of fire lookout stations under construction and a lot of catching up to be done in the telephone line and trail construction that had been interrupted the previous year by the fires. The Forest Service bought more mules for the North Fork. Taylor Valarde was hired as an extra packer. The fall of 1930, he went back south to Arizona, where we heard that he was later killed in a knife fight.

During the summer, I had the pleasure of taking out on a backcountry inspection trip several officials from the regional office and the supervisor's office. Included was Mr. K.D. Swan, who was, along with his other duties, the official regional photographer. The following year, he would be included in a similar group that I took out in the far reaches of the St. Joe and Clearwater National Forests in Idaho.

The last year that I saw a sawbuck saddle in the National Forests was 1929. They were still in use in Glacier Park however, and between 1948 and 1952, when I worked at Grand Canyon National Park, the Fred Harvey Company, the Park concessionaire, still used them. During that period, they purchased at least eighteen new sawbucks. From what I could find out when I packed in Idaho, the Decker saddle being used there, designed by the Decker brothers, had come into use at about the time of the 1910 fires.

There was a lot of packing in the Idaho panhandle because the almost vertical mountainsides were just too steep for road building. The contract packer thrived here because the mining companies and large lumber concerns such as Weyerhaeuser, Diamond Match and Ohio Match had to depend on pack train transportation to supply their industry.

Contract or Gyppo packers such as the Stonebreakers, Noel and Riley Farrel, Bobby Stauffer and dozens of others owned the best of pack stock and equipped them, of course, with Decker saddles. The men who packed these strings became true experts at this trade because they worked practically the whole year and were called upon to transport all kinds of freight, including every conceivable type of machinery.

One evening, when I returned from a pack trip, the Forest Supervisor, William Nagel, and a couple of the rangers from other districts were at the station. A little while later, they called me in and showed me a letter, a copy of which had gone to all Forest Supervisors in the Northern Region. The letter stated that in view of the importance of pack train transportation in this huge region of Montana, Idaho and Eastern Washington, more study was to be made to see if there was any way in which this part of the Forest Service operation could be improved upon.

Region One already had their forests equipped with the best pack stock and equipment that money could buy, and packers were required to pack 250 pounds per mule. It had been "ascertained" that a packer could not handle more than nine mules effectively; on the other hand, if he were packing less than nine he was not earning his pay. This circular letter told that a packers' contest was to be held at the newly established Forest Service Remount Depot near Huson, near US Highway 10. Each Forest

Supervisor was instructed to get together with his rangers and select a representative packer to be sent to this convention. Top officials of the region, as well as any other Forest officers with a wide knowledge of packing, would also be present. It also stated that since this meeting was to end with a nine-mule packing contest, it behooved them to give thought to selecting their best packers.

One was always hearing that here, or perhaps there, was the best packer in the region, or that this or that man was the fastest packer in the business. Now the best would have a chance to compete against the best in a full string contest, judged by men who had been around packing and had done it all their working lives.

They advised me that I had been selected to represent the Blackfeet Forest at this meeting and contest. The alternate ranger and commissary clerk had learned of my selection before me and had even told others in the district of it over the telephone. Word spread rapidly throughout the district, and soon my loyal compatriots were assuring me that I would surely win it—that I couldn't possibly be beaten. Many had worked in other forests and assured me that they had never seen a man who could come close to me in cargoing, speed—you name it. To one and all I had the same answer: "I only hope that I don't place last." With my youthful confidence and enthusiasm, I knew that I could do the job faster and maybe better than the average, but then I knew that the fellows I would be going up against would not be the average. Many of them would be selected from among thirty packers in their forests.

Rolf Fremming, who was now the Upper North Fork district ranger, chose to take time off and attend as a spectator. I rode with him in his automobile. The Remount Depot had been established only that year, and the pack strings they had on hand at the time were half-broken three- and four-year-olds, all range-raised and as wild as a herd of elk in captivity. At the depot we were assigned bunks in tents set up for the occasion.

There were eighteen of us who officially entered. The depot, which had more than a dozen packers, had one entry, and the other seventeen of us were from the various forests. Two of the entries were cargo men, and some of the packers thought they should be barred because of the fact they got so much more practice. They spent their entire time cargoing loads and helping packers load and did not spend any time at all with stock. When asked how I felt about it, I said that I thought if any man could beat a packer at packing, he had the right to be declared the winner. Later, one of these cargo men, Swede Cummings of the Clearwater National Forest, dropped out of the contest when he got a look at the unruly stock and the conditions of the contest. Two other packers, Andy Kirk of the Flathead and Plummer of the Missoula Forest, also dropped out before the contest.

As the conversation went along, the best ways of doing each phase of the operation were discussed, and different arguments and demonstrations were presented. All of us learned something, as to each there had been some phase that had given him trouble, but each time there emerged one in the group that had the answer. Practically all of them were ten or twelve years older than I, and most had spent the greater part of their lives working as Gyppo packers, working practically the year 'round and packing everything that needed moving. I doubt that anybody learned more in that week than I did. My eyes and ears were wide open to everything that was said and done. I felt that I learned more in that week than I had in my three years of packing for the Forest Service. I had made an effort always to learn as much as I could from every man I came in contact with, but here I was learning every hour, from the best.

For the contest, a twenty-five-man firefighting outfit was chosen. Four six-foot crosscut saws had to be packed across the loads, axes, Pulaskis, equipment boxes and rations, tent flies and Kimmel stoves. The "rations" were a mixture of sawdust and gravel in ration boxes. The heaviest side packs were 135 pounds, no heavier than all of us were used to packing. When loaded, the packer's string was to be led a half mile across the meadow, around a hay shed and back. The five judges, all with packing experience in their own right, would ride beside the string and give their scores on the cargoing and the manner in which the loads rode. Since the stock was all newly broken, and each and every animal was likely to buck with its pack, it was required that we tie each side pack down to the cinch ring. One packer eventually cheated by merely running the sling ropes down through the rigging rings beforehand, thus saving much time, and made the fastest time of the contest. Several of the contestants grumbled about this and were going to call it to the attention of the judges but did not. I don't see how the five judges could have missed it and wondered why they had not penalized this man.

The judges were Rangers Ed McKay of the Lolo National Forest, Dean Harrington of the Coeur d'Alene National Forest and Neil Smith of Flathead Forest and Supervisors W.F. Buckingham of Clearwater and J.C. Urquhardt of the Selway National Forest. Cargoing and loading nine mule loads requires a lot of moves and much exertion. Doing it against time, and with this kind of audience, added to the stress. Many referred to it afterward as an endurance contest. As an example, Tommy Thompson, a six-foot-two, 200-pounder, was wearing a blue broadcloth shirt, and when finished, there was not a dry spot

*This page*: Held at the U.S. Forest Service Ninemile Remount Depot at Huson, Montana, the 1930 Northern Region Packer's Contest is believed to have been the only full-string (nine-mule) packing contest ever held.

as large as the palm of his hand on it. I recall that he slapped his thigh as he finished, saying, "Never again." As he did so, the drops of sweat flew through the air from between his fingers.

During the contest, the Kootenai Forest packer got overheated and ill and had to drop out. Because of these mules being only partly halter broken and could not be led by a man on foot, and the fact that they might pull away from him while being led, each of us was furnished a wrangler on horseback to assist in getting them to the loading point and then to where they would be tailed on to the string. It was also decided to use a "squeeze" made of two fourteen-foot poles fastened to the hitchrail three feet apart. The pole on the right of the mule was anchored securely to the ground at its lower end by a stout stake. The other pole was attached to a rope. This left side pole would be moved out away from the other to form a sort of funnel. When the animal was between the poles, the left one was then pulled inward with the rope until it was parallel with the first. The mule was then between the two poles, which were three feet apart. This greatly slowed the packer and hampered him in balancing his loads, but at least it permitted him to get to the mule with the side pack and to lash it on without having his legs kicked from under him.

A possible 25 points were to be given for the manner in which the loads were cargoed and for neatness. An additional 25 possible points were given for speed. The fastest man was to be given 25, the slowest 12.5 and the others prorated between. Then 50 points would be given for the manner in which the loads rode during the trip across the meadow and around the hay shed. Because of the great amount of lumber packing and camp moves I had had, I had gotten in the habit of wearing gloves all the time while packing. During the contest I wore them all the way, and I'm quite sure I was the only one to do so.

My time for the contest was 50:5.9. The eventual winner, Guy Woodworth of the Coeur d'Alene National Forest, took 49:18.8, and P.H. (Tommy) Thompson of the Nez Perce Forest in placing second took 49:34.2. The three slowest times were 61:0.5, 64:20.4 and 64:40.7. Woodworth, in winning, was given a score of 94.0 points. They gave me 85.5. Only four of the packers made scores of less than 80. I had drawn string no. 1, and after I had finished loading, and before starting to lead them out, Rolf Fremming, who had been a timer for one of the other strings, said, "Bill, I think you've got a chance for first."

I looked across at string no. 3, which Guy Woodworth had just finished loading, and again said, "I only hope I don't finish in last place." I realized how easy it would be in this company.

Right after that, Andy Kirk, a Flathead packer and one of those who had dropped out and who was now assigned as my wrangler on horseback, asked me, "What'll you take for the chaps, kid?" (A pair of chaps was being given the winner.) Again I came up with my only wish.

Well, I didn't finish last; in fact, I finished in the first division, as they say in big-league baseball, but I will always feel honored to have been a part of that select group. Guy Woodworth came and shook my hand and said, "Kid,

The author greatly enjoyed and certainly related to this Charles M. Russell sketch of a pair of packers throwing a diamond hitch. *Charles M. Russell, public domain.*

if you had drawn any string other than number one, you'd have given me a run for my money."

In the end, when Regional Director Evan W. Kelly made the presentations, in his speech he said in part, "Never at any time anywhere has there been assembled a group of packers as good as these I am looking at right now."

At the start of this meeting, it had been the intention to raise the required load limit per mule from 250 to 300 pounds. We packers as a group succeeded in convincing the officials that 250 was as high as it should ever be. Also, as a result of this meeting, some changes were made in the Decker saddle and other equipment.

This was to be the only official full-string packers' contest ever to be held. In retrospect I pondered, as one will, that had I drawn string no. 2 or no. 3, I might have placed third, as string no. 1 became notorious for crowding and bucking. The 45 I was given for the riding of my loads was the highest given anyone using string no. 1, whereas scores of 50 were made on the other two—but then, I didn't finish last! My score of 85.5 put me in the top half of the group.

At the close of the contest, the Kaniksu Forest packer, Haskins, made an exhibition ride on an unused mule, and the Bitterroot packer, McCormick, and I gave rope spinning exhibitions.

While I was at the packers' contest, I received a telephone call from Mrs. McNelly. S.L. McNelly had passed away, and she wanted to get Sam, that magnificent saddle animal that I had used and cared for as my own for the past two years, back to her parents' ranch at Potomac, Montana. Since I was to be at the Remount Depot a few days longer, the best I could do was to give her the name of the place he was at the time, Home Ranch Bottoms, where he was with the Forest Service stock, and the names of, and how to locate, those who would help in getting him for her.

I never saw Sam again.

The author (*second from left*) and his coworkers at their tent cabin in Avery, Idaho, in 1931.

Permanent structures at the base of a steep hillside in Avery. *National Archives*.

*Chapter 5*

# PACKING IN THE IDAHO PANHANDLE

In talking with the other packers at the Remount Depot, I learned that the $110 a month I was making in packing for the Blackfoot National Forest was as much as anyone except for those in the St. Joe Forest. There were some packers over there who were making $115. During that winter, the Blackfeet Forest announced a 10 percent "economy" deduction in all wages. Recalling that St. Joe was known to pay highest, I wrote their supervisor's office applying for a job there. As I had bested their top man in the contest by more than fourteen minutes, and by four points, I made sure I told them I had been there. (Not mentioning their own man, of course.) Jobs were mighty scarce in those days and Idaho had lots of packers who were out of work, but I was offered a job without delay. Later that summer, I learned that at Big Creek three packers had been hired to do the district packing that I had handled alone for three seasons. There surely must have been a heavier workload, but I really razzed them about it afterward.

The supervisor's office was located at St. Maries on the St. Joe River, but Avery, forty-five miles farther up the river, was the main hub of activity. It was to Avery that I was instructed to report. I did not realize until I arrived at Avery that until just prior to that, the mainline of the Milwaukee Road (the Chicago, Milwaukee, St. Paul and Pacific Railroad), which passed through there between Spokane and Missoula, had been their only connection with the outside world.

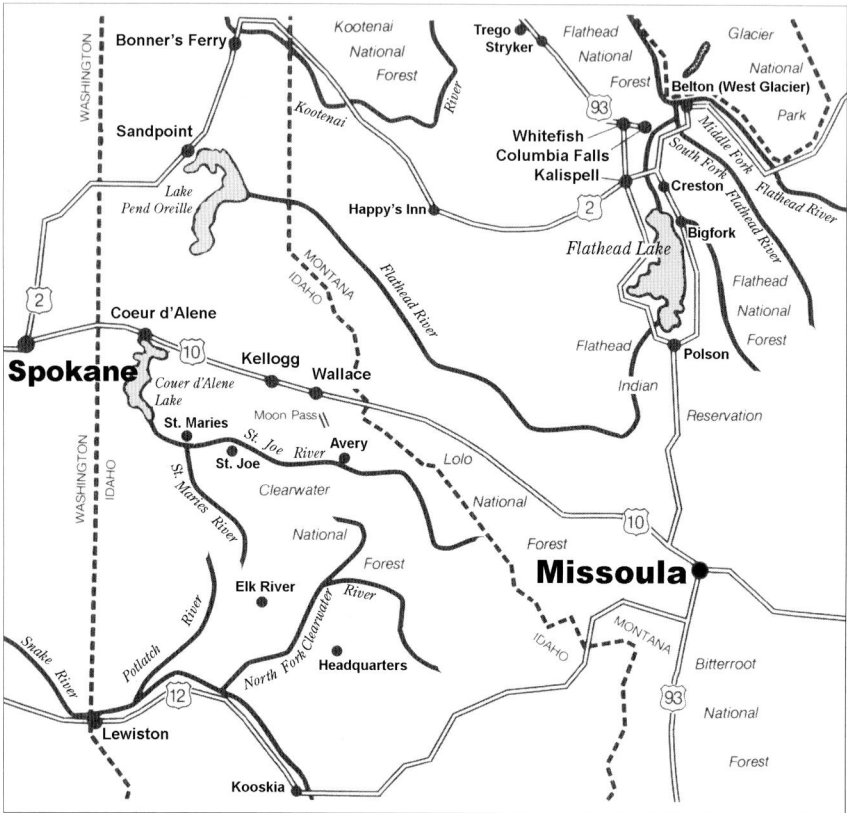

This map shows the areas where the author worked in the Idaho panhandle in relation to adjacent areas of Washington and northwestern Montana. Note the author's home stomping grounds north of Flathead Lake.

It was told that during the terrible fires of 1910, which hit this area harder than any, Milwaukee trains had been forced to wait in tunnels until the worst of the fire had passed. On Slate Creek, near Avery, eighty-five men had perished in a group. At a location not far away, a forest ranger named Pulaski had held his crew in a mine shaft at the point of a gun while the fire passed and had himself been temporarily blinded as a result of being near the entrance of the mine. While he was blind, two men had managed to slip past him. Their bodies were found less than a quarter of a mile from the mine. Pulaski, like Bosworth, was an inventor. One of his inventions, named for him, is the best known. It is like a cross between a mattock and an axe and is universally the most frequently used hand tool used in fighting forest fires.

I had heard that there was a road from Wallace to Avery over Moon Pass. I did not know until I got to it that it was just a newly constructed bulldozer trail. In Wallace I had to ask a lot of people before I finally found one who knew where this trail took off from US Highway 10. It was a steep grade out of Wallace and except for an occasional turnout was only one vehicle wide. It seemed to take me hours to drive to the top of Moon Pass, and since the surrounding timber was second growth since the 1910 fire, it was as thick as could be. As I neared the top, I met three men in an old truck with a load of firewood. My right-hand side of the road was levelable ground, then the town continued on the other side, which from this point had a little inhabitable space.

I drove along this row of small houses for a couple hundred yards, then suddenly the road before me became a smooth black cinder road. I was about to speed up, since this was the first decent stretch of road I had seen for hours, when a man wearing a deputy sheriff's badge stepped out in the "road" and held up his hand, palm toward me. I stopped, and he asked me where I thought I was going. I told him I was headed for Avery. He said, "You're there now. In fact, you are on the train station platform."

I had missed a sharp turn in the dirt road at the end of the platform during my consternation at seeing the sudden improvement in the road condition. I backed up to this bend and after that had only about fifty yards to go to get to the Forest headquarters.

My Model A Ford caused no less stir in Avery than Lindbergh's plane had in Paris a few years before. It really amazed me how the people gathered 'round it and stared, asking questions about my "trip," how much the Model A cost, where I was going to keep it during the spring and summer, etc. They all had to touch every part of it, and it later occurred to me that probably some of the old Gyppo packers in the group were figuring out how they would get it into pieces that could be packed into the backcountry on a mule.

The Forest Service complex was off to one side, up a steep ravine. I drove up there and found a place to park the car. Two of the forest rangers, Charlie Scribner and Wilfred Renshaw, had been among the crowd I had attracted down on the road, which was at that point Avery's only street. They showed me where I would bunk, got my employment papers processed and told me that I would be shown my pack string the next morning. The animals had already been shod, and I was told that my first trip would be to take a telephone line construction camp to Broken Leg Cabin, seventy-five miles up the river.

The U.S. Forest Service North Fork Ranger District Building in Avery, Idaho, at the time that the author knew it. *National Archives.*

That evening, I "took in the town," what there was of it. The street I had left continued about one hundred yards, downriver, and then ended because of the steep side hill reaching to the river's edge. There it crossed by way of a suspension bridge, suspended on stout cables. This bridge was capable of supporting a loaded pack string, which could weigh upward of six tons. Later, when the snows on the St. Joe–Clearwater Divide had melted, and truck-trail construction had got underway, the two-ton truck that started hauling our materials out eight or ten miles had no difficulty in crossing the bridge. As mentioned, on the other side of the bridge the town continued for another quarter of a mile, with structures in single file because of the narrowness of the flat. At Avery, the Milwaukee Railroad changed from steam to electricity, so there were a great number of railroad employees living here. The Terriault brothers had a drugstore, and the White Mercantile was the large general store. There was even a barbershop.

Up at the ranger station, the cookhouse was in operation so I had a good supper. Farther up the ravine was the huge, forty-head barn and the corrals. The barn had a ramp that allowed a truck to drive into its loft. This barn was famous far and wide because of its size and top-quality construction. Unfortunately, it was to burn in the summer of 1965. The next morning I was shown where I could put my suitcase and packsack for safe keeping. I was introduced to my pack string, which proved to be fully as large, or even larger on an average, than my first string at Big Creek. They had never been together as a string before, and I was to learn that they were very much mismatched at the beginning.

I was told later that the man in charge of the stock had not been particularly happy about a Montana man coming and taking a job he felt should have been given to a local one. Therefore, he was much less than cooperative in giving me any of the information about the animals, equipment, places and things I would have liked to have. I learned later that two of the mules, Speck and Eel, had been rejected by two or three packers because they were considered "knot heads" that could not be taught anything and were hard to catch. I was to go as far as Nugget Creek that day, a distance of eighteen miles up the river. By the time I got my string saddled and to the warehouse, my nine mule loads were cargoed. They were extremely heavy, averaged 285 pounds per mule, but were expertly cargoed.

The head cargo man, Arnold Harrington, brother of Dean Harrington (a Coeur d'Alene ranger and a judge at the packer's contest), was as good at his job as any man I have ever seen. He had, of course, the advantage of a smooth floor to work on, scales to weigh materials on, plenty of time and, last but not least of the advantages, mostly full cases and sacks to work with. Sugar, potatoes, oats and all such sacked items came in 125-pound sacks, so all the cargo men had to do with them was wrap them up. Cases of string beans, corn, etc., with number two cans were cargoed three to a pack, while canned fruit and other items in cans, and weighing 60 pounds, were packed two to a side.

At Nugget Creek, there was no grass as yet, so we fed hay to our stock. The second day, another eighteen miles upriver I turned my stock loose to graze for the night. There were no bell mares in Idaho, just nine mules and your saddle horse. The next morning, I found it impossible to catch Speck and Eel. (I began to suspect why the name Eel.) No enticing with the nosebag would allow me to get close to them. My saddle horse, Bally, a large bald-faced bay, proved to be a wonderful string horse, but as a roping horse, he was no better than being afoot. I saw that the mules could outrun him, so that I never would be able to get close enough to throw a rope. By this time, they had sort of established a path in which they circled through the timber, so I set a snare between two trees using two half-inch sling ropes for double strength, fastened high enough where it was anchored to give spring to it, like a fly rod. This worked perfectly; in fact, Speck ended up stretched full length with the two ropes so tight that I had to cut them at the eye to keep him from strangling. I made sure I had his halter on first, and the halter rope anchored. That is the last time I ever had trouble catching either of them.

In a few days, the worst mules I had were the gentlest ones, as they were the ones that did not lead well but rather kept their halter ropes taut a great deal of the time. My third overnight stop was at Bean Creek, where Ranger Haun and his crew in 1910 had been mentioned in the Spokane and Seattle newspapers as having perished in the forest fire.

The fourth day out, I reached Broken Leg Cabin. The crew that was to use the camp I was packing in had left Avery a few days before and had maintained telephone lines to Nugget Creek, then to Red Ives—my second night's stop, where I had snared the mules—then to Midget Creek, Timber Creek and so on. When I got to Broken Leg, they were about a half hour behind me, as I had passed them in the early afternoon. After I had looked the grazing situation over and put up a trail barricade in one location, I returned to the cabin and got acquainted with the crew. I was comparatively fresh after four fairly short days of packing, and they were pretty weary, so I told them that I'd get supper. (Broken Leg Cabin was seventy-eight miles by trail from Avery.)

The Forest Service did not furnish bread to any of its crews in those days, but lots of baking powder, yeast and flour. I decided to make baking powder biscuits for supper and, in the interest of time, just put the batter in the bake pan from the spoon—drop biscuits we called them. When it was ready, I called them and they fell to. I didn't start to eat for a little while, as I was getting a dessert ready, putting dishwater on the stove, cutting more wood and other tasks.

A little while after I sat down to eat, I picked up one of my biscuits, which were the prettiest golden brown of any I'd ever made, broke it in two, buttered it with Blanchard's canned butter and took a bite. It was about the foulest tasting thing I had ever eaten. I immediately looked around the table and saw that each of the fellows had eaten half a biscuit. I told them not to eat any more and asked them whether they had noticed the foul odor and taste. Jack Howell, the foreman of the crew, said they

The author, seen here in 1931, leading a pack string across the St. Joe River near the mouth of Timber Creek, fifty-five miles upriver from Avery in the St. Joe National Forest.

had, but since I had been good enough to bake them, they didn't feel like saying anything. Upon investigation, we discovered that some meat had been left in the oven the previous fall and that it had spoiled. The closed oven had held the stench, and it had then permeated the biscuits.

Some ten miles downriver from the Broken Leg Cabin, I had passed Bean Creek. Miners had built flumes to carry water for their placer mining. Bean Creek, like most of the streams in that part of Idaho, had a small amount of gold in its gravel streambed. There was a small portable sawmill situated there that Gyppo packers had packed over the Bitterroot Mountains from the Montana side, probably from a trailhead between St. Regis and Superior. Gyppo packers had been doing business in those mountains since the turn of the century, servicing mines, logging operations and hunting parties.

Another packer named Lloyd Henderson, like myself, had been given a string of very large mules. He had been working for the St. Joe Forest a few years, all in the Twin Peaks district. Since more of my main line packing was routed on the St. Joe–Clearwater Divide than up the river trail, my first two days' travel were through his district, and we always seemed to be going the same direction and at the same time, at least as far as Bearskull patrol cabin, an overnight stop. He had once been a big-time rodeo saddle bronc rider. In packing with him I learned that he was in the habit of setting his packs lower, like I always had done. When we loaded out together, we would go the distance of our daily miles without having to adjust a single pack. In our loading out practice, the man whose string was being loaded would tighten the cinch and then take down the sling rope.

By that time, the pack he was going to tie on the left side had been boosted by the other so that it was setting crosswise on top of the packsaddle. He would let it slide down into place and tie it. He would then get the loop of the other man's sling rope ready, and when the right side pack had been boosted in place, he would flip this loop around the pack so that all the man on the right had to do was make his tie and flip the top loop over to the first man. Time after time I timed us at thirteen minutes to load out the eighteen mules. Like the other packers in Idaho, he was very independent, not liking any official very well and not cooperating as well with the foremen and men of the crews as I had been in the habit of doing.

One day, Henderson and I had just arrived at the end of the road where our eighteen loads were waiting when Supervisor Myrick and the head of the Spokane warehouse drove up. Eldon H. Myrick had been a ranger in my home area for many years. The North Fork, Java, Essex, Spotted Bear and the Swan Lake area had been some of his assignments, and such names as Art Halvorson, Henry Thol, Ansley Hutchinson, Jim Ready and George Steppler were familiar to us in common. He always liked to chat with me when an opportunity came.

That day, the man from Spokane, Jim Terry, asked Eldon Myrick how long it would take us to load the huge stack of packs on eighteen mules. Myrick answered, "We can time them," and winked at me. Being young and enthusiastic, I said to Henderson, "Let's show them how fast we can load out." He was older and less of a showoff, so he said, "To hell with them. I wouldn't speed up for any of those types." It took us exactly fifteen minutes. Both were amazed.

The St. Joe National Forest personnel were extremely proud of their livestock, and justly so, as most of their pack strings were of matched mules. Muggs Bentley packed the "Midget String," all small mules, while Peter Manring the "Black String," mules all of the same size and all coal black. Two of them looked so much alike that I was unable to tell them apart, and as we would load out together, I usually called the name of the other when referring to one. Finally, one day I noticed a small clipped patch on the left side of one's neck. Pete confessed that he had done this each spring

A view of the schoolhouse in Avery, Idaho, with the St. Joe River in the background. Note the dead timber from the 1910 fires. *National Archives.*

in order that he, their packer, could tell which was which. Don Cressler led, or "pulled," a string of nine gray mules and rode a gray saddle horse. Andy Oliver and Oral "Pop" Flynn had roans and sorrels, and so on. Henderson and I just had "big" mules.

In spite of their inborn distrust (and dislike) for a packer from another state, as well as a sort of clannishness, when I was loading out at an overnight stop with just one of the Idaho packers, they were not unfriendly. I know that behind my back they probably referred to me as a "sheep herder" because I was from Montana, just as a Washingtonian was an "apple knocker" or a Californian a "prune picker." Occasionally, there were a few jibes and caustic remarks but nothing serious. One morning at Elk Prairie Ranger Station, I was to make a trip within the district, and I had all my loads cargoed and setting on the warehouse platform. I had watered my stock at the small water trough, which by then was nearly empty. Flynn followed me to the water trough, and as I was pulling away, he said, "As soon as I water my string I'll help you load out."

He had to wait for the trough to fill so that by the time he had finished watering, I had loaded my string and had mounted my horse. He was surprised and said, "What the hell, Bill, you loaded out already?" I said, "Well, it's not unusual for a Montana man to pack his string while an Idaho guy is watering his." He laughed and said, "Well you're pretty good, but you will have to spend a winter on Salmon River before you will be considered a good packer in Idaho."

The tallest mule in my outfit was a white mule named Kaiser. He was within an inch or less of eighteen hands, or six feet, at the withers. He might not have weighed as much as some of the others, but he had a big, rawboned frame and an enormous appetite. His stomach was always in a receptive mood. At times when I was staying overnight where the grazing was scant, I would feed an extra-large feed of oats to the mules. I noticed that Kaiser was the only one that never left any grain in his nosebag, even when he had had a double feed. Even then he would act as though he wanted more. I remarked about this to Henderson a couple of times, and he told me that one of his mules, Gimlet, who was nearly as tall as Kaiser, was the same way. I had often said that Kaiser could eat more oats than any mule alive, but one day Henderson said he thought Gimlet could out eat them all, including Kaiser.

We got to talking as the mules ate and found that we each had about fifty cents in change in our pockets, so we decided to have a contest, winner takes all. We gave each of them a second gallon, which was promptly cleaned up. We then put a carefully measured half gallon in each nosebag with the same results. It began to look like this could go on all afternoon, so we added a second half gallon. Kaiser made no attempt to take even one small bite, just stood and looked at me as if to say, "Get this bag off me."

Gimlet ate most of his, a total of nearly three gallons of rolled oats! I might mention that a mule will not grain founder or water founder himself as a horse will.

One trip I was on my way to the end of the road and was staying overnight at Bearskull. Two of the longtime St. Joe packers were on their way in the opposite direction with loaded strings and also staying overnight there. During the evening, the ranger alternate from the station up the trail twenty miles away phoned and asked them if they would stop at Twin Lakes cabin and pick up a wooden wall telephone that was on the table there and bring it with them the next day. I was not surprised when both refused, saying that their strings were fully loaded and they had no empty animal to pack it on. The phone was light and would have been no trouble whatever, but they were like that sometimes. On my return with my loads, I was again staying at Bearskull, and the same alternate phoned me with the same request.

I said, "Slim, I was here the other evening when two of your old-time Idaho packers refused to pick up that phone. Now I have to live and work with those fellows, and while I know as well as you do that your request is not an unreasonable one, I'll have to turn you down, as much as I dislike doing so."

He fully understood, and the next day when I arrived at Twin Lakes, he was there, riding the ranger's horse with the little phone packed on the "office mule."

There was one place up the St. Joe River where there were bad bogs. One place in particular had become practically impassable as the deep mule tracks filled with water and got deeper. After having to pull three mules out of it, wading in, unpacking them and carrying the packs out in mud more than knee deep, I found a detour place fifty yards up the slope where I could cross. I had asked the ranger a number of times if he would have the small line construction crew, camped only a couple of miles from there, corduroy it. He said that he could leave them in the area only long enough to finish the phone line to Needle Peak, that there would be no time for corduroying.

On my next trip past this place, I knew that the ranger and the assistant supervisor were less than an hour behind me and would be staying at the same place I would that night. When I made my detour of that bog, up the hillside and back into the trail, I went back and carefully erased all sign that would indicate my having left the trail. I was at the cabin where we were to spend the night, and when they arrived, I was gratified to see that their horses and saddles were muddy right up to the seats of the saddles and the horses showed signs of having fallen on their sides in the bog. That evening, the ranger phoned the telephone crew foreman and instructed him to corduroy the boghole.

Late in the 1931 season, a difference of opinion, or something, developed between the ranger and one of the packers, which resulted in the latter being discharged. His string was turned out at Elk Prairie, where they would often come to the ranger station and stand around during the day, fighting flies. Often, while graining my own stock, I would give them a feed of oats. There was a mare with this string, and of course the mules were never far from her side. On one overnight stay there, I recalled that as I arrived I had seen the mules in a ravine, but that the mare had not been visible. The next morning as I was bringing my own stock to the corral, I again saw the mules but not the mare. While feeding and saddling my stock, one of the mules came out of the ravine and almost to the corral, braying all the while, then went back into the ravine. After breakfast, as I was preparing to start on my day's trip, this same thing again took place. The same mule would approach nearly to the corral, constantly braying, then turn and go into the ravine. I had a long trip ahead of me and had no time to investigate, but I told the alternate and the foreman of a small crew that were working out of the station that I thought it should be investigated.

In the ravine they found the mare mired in a bog. She had fallen over on one side and was exhausted from her struggles. In checking the spot when I got back to Elk Prairie, it appeared to me that she might have been able to extricate herself had she not mired straddle lengthwise of a six-inch lodgepole log that was beneath the mud. With the help of the ranger's saddle horse that I had saddled and left in the corral for them, the five men were able to get her out, but she was unable to stand and died within an hour. Every time I ever looked at that mule after that I got a lump in my throat. The poor cuss sure had tried hard to tell me.

IN THE SUMMER OF 1931, during the forest fires, I worked for about three weeks with a packer who owned his own string and was packing them, hired out to the Clearwater Forest. Years back he had been a well-known football player for the University of Idaho. He was six feet seven and weighed 275. His name was Chet Coburn. He was one of the finest gentlemen I've ever worked with, and of course with his size and strength, he was a good man to pack with. We became very close friends in the time we were together. He never could, however, get used to the early hour that I got him up in the morning. The stock, upon being turned loose, would normally stand around for a couple of hours and rest, then saunter off and find the place they wanted to graze.

The author fording the St. Joe River at Avery in 1931 with a pack string with lumber loads. The suspension bridge in the background was under repair.

After having eaten their fill, they would lie down until just as dawn was breaking. Then, not being particularly hungry, they would usually start to ramble. We found that it saved us many hours of hiking after them if we were where they were when this time came. Therefore, we would get up about four and pick up their tracks. Of course we always watched which direction they took the afternoon before.

One morning when we were staying at a camp where I knew good grazing to be close by and that the stock always came in to the corral in the morning, I told Chet, "We will sleep until 5:30 tomorrow morning." He was happy and said he hated to be sneaking up on those poor old mules in the dark.

Chet had two mules that looked exactly alike, but there the resemblance ended—one was gentle, with a friendly disposition, while the other was about as mean as they come. It was hard to catch, so Chet left the halter on it all the time. It did not lead well, so he had a chain on the halter to go under the mule's chin. One morning we had got our stock into the corral, which at this camp was on a hillside. While Chet was attempting to fasten the halter rope to the halter of this mule, the mule suddenly dragged his chain across the back of the mule Chet was reaching across. The back of Chet's hand was badly lacerated by the chain. I told him to go to the ranger station for first aid and that the other packers and I would catch and feed his stock meanwhile. This bronky mule had run in between two mules that were tied up, so I decided to go up on the left side of the mule and try to grab the halter. I was never without gloves on my hands when doing this type of work.

As I approached the rear of the mule on the left, he suddenly decided to move to the left, leaving a clear path from the mean mule's heels to my belly. It was on the lower side of the corral, and I was going downhill, making it difficult to back up. I stepped to the left and his foot caught me on the right short ribs. I fell against the rear of the mule on the left, which luckily was a gentle one. Immediately another Clearwater packer, Alva Wilson from Weippe, Idaho, grabbed me and helped me to the platform our saddles were stacked on. He was greatly agitated, fearing that I was seriously injured. As soon as I could get a little wind, I whispered hoarsely, "I'm not hurt." He said, "The hell you aren't. You're hurt, and you're hurt bad." I got a little air in me and whispered, "Just got the wind knocked out of me." At that, Alva at last began to breathe more freely himself.

Shortly after I arrived at Avery, Charlie Scribner, one of the rangers, approached me one day and wanted to make a deal to rent my Model A for the summer. It was evident that I would have no chance to use it, so I consented to his terms of ten cents a mile, with him furnishing the gas and oil. The only place he could drive, except over Moon Pass, was up the river eight miles to Gold Creek that summer on picnics. He made at least one trip over Moon Pass and back. When I arrived at Avery at the end of the packing season, Charlie told me, "Bill, I don't think my family are going to let you take that Model A out of Avery."

I got hold of a *Spokesman Review* newspaper at the bunkhouse and got an idea of what they were selling for in Spokane (and added a little for bringing it over Moon Pass), and we made a deal. The snow was low on the hillsides, and I didn't feel much like a drive over Moon Pass in the snow.

During the time I packed for the Forest Service in Idaho, there were at least twice that thirty nine-mule strings loaded out at one pack station in one day. One was at Avery when packing for the Simmons Ridge fire. There were nineteen strings loaded out in the morning and an additional eleven shortly after noon. I can't recall the names of many of the remount packers, but one was Slim Johnson and another was Monte Peyton, whose brother, Hugh, would be my immediate supervisor the next year in Glacier National Park.

In Slim's string were two mules that he always seemed to be having trouble with. They were named Gray Goose and Rimrock Nell. He was constantly screaming at them. I had become very well acquainted with

Slim, and because he had packed in my district and the adjoining one, we had been together at overnight stops and had loaded out together on many occasions. I was nearly kicked a dozen times by Rimrock Nell, who I spoke of as "Rimfire." Slim was very noisy around his stock, with lots of screaming and shouting, which was considered poor practice, but his stock seemed to get used to it.

The saddle horse, Bally, was a very good string horse but could be very hard to catch in the woods in the morning. A couple of times when my stock had "rambled" and I had to walk nine miles to get them, I was unable to catch him and had to walk an additional nine miles chasing them back to the corral. One morning, six or eight of us were at the same station, a place where there was good graze a little more than a mile from the corrals. Bally had been particularly hard to catch, so when we started to walk up the mountain after our stock, I didn't bother to take my bridle and the nosebag used to entice the saddle horse. That morning, however, I walked right up to Bally. As we started back down the mountain, some of the other fellows were afoot, some had caught their mounts. I hopped on Bally and was riding along bareback behind the loose stock, talking with some of

The Elk Prairie Ranger Station in the St. Joe National Forest, forty-one miles from the nearest road at Avery. Note the dead timber from the 1910 fires.

93

the others, when without warning Bally broke into a mad gallop down the steep hillside. He was going too fast for me to bail off on that rocky slope, and in order to get hold of his bell, I would have had to risk going off over his head because of the incline of his back. I couldn't sit upright because of the sturdy tree limbs under which we were passing. I just sort of slid back, got a good hold of his mane and decided to ride it out.

He had passed all of the seventy or eighty other animals long before reaching the corral, but now a new danger confronted me—or us. The corral gate was on the left side of the corral as we approached it, and I couldn't see how he could possibly turn into it without breaking both our necks. He started to slow down when we were about fifty feet from the gate, but with our speed and the downslope, I could see that he would never get slowed down enough. Guess he realized it, too, as he then speeded up again and ran on past, to the water trough, where he came to a screeching halt and proceeded to drink. I just sat on him and laughed. The pranks animals at times play on us humans always amuse me.

Elk Prairie Ranger Station was located on the St. Joe–Clearwater Divide at a fairly high elevation, about three thousand feet higher than the St. Joe River and six miles distant by way of the Timber Creek Trail. This entire area is a part of the famous 1910 burn that is so well described by Betty Goodwin Spencer in her book, *The Big Blowup*. Hillsides were laced with fallen, fire-killed timber. One day after a hard rain, I was going down the Timber Creek Trail to the river when a pack in midstring bumped the lower end of a fallen tree. This tree immediately slid downhill, knocking that mule off the trail. As he fell, he pulled the mule ahead of him off balance, and that mule also fell off the trail. The mule behind attempted to jump the windfall and met the same fate. The fallen timber was so thickly laced that all three mules rolled over it several feet before falling straight down among the tree trunks to land some ten feet below the top logs. I went down among the logs and loosed the cinches on all the mules, tied up all of the stock still on the trail and then hiked the three and a half miles back to the ranger station, where luckily there was a three-man crew cutting firewood. They accompanied me back to the site of the wreck, where we cut the timber away and rescued the stock. Aside from some minor abrasions they were not injured.

The first work for the packers after fall rains commence is to bring the men and their equipment from the lookouts. Unless they are students, returning to school, they are assigned to a crew building bridges, lookout towers, trails or phone lines. When the snows start coming to the mountains to stay, all of those crews are brought in. Stock are unshod and taken to winter range.

As the snow got deeper in the mountain passes, I began to think of my trip over Moon Pass several months before with my Model A Ford. I wondered if the pass might be closed for the winter.

Since my Model A Ford was now Charlie Scribner's Model A Ford, I went to Spokane by train and got my first real look at the "Great Depression." Some bread lines were a block and a half long. I guess I thought of myself as the richest man in Spokane.

W.J. Yenne at Siyeh Pass in Glacier National Park, riding the saddle horse known as Dude. This animal was the favorite mount of Glacier chief engineer Charles E. Randels.

## Chapter 6

# WORKING IN GLACIER NATIONAL PARK

I learned many things during my work in Idaho, working with St. Joe and Clearwater Forest Service personnel, especially the packers. I also learned much about the management and techniques of suppressing large forest fires. The Flathead National Forest had a fire control officer through the 1960s named Frank Meneely, especially in 1967 on the Flathead Fire, which was on the Glacier Park side of North Fork of the Flathead River. One day, Shorty and I were talking about old times on forest fires and I mentioned fires I had been on in the Clearwater Forest in 1931. I told him of incidents and of men I had worked with there. He said, "Hell, Bill, we must have been within ten feet of each other a number of times."

Since much of my work has been connected with backcountry pack transportation, both as a packer in the beginning and then in a supervisory capacity, I might mention that from the very beginning packing and its various styles and different types of equipment have intrigued me.

Therefore I've made a sort of study of it. In Region One of the U.S. Forest Service, the Decker packsaddle had been adopted and the old sawbuck with its various diamond hitches had been discarded. Old-time methods and history were of a high interest to me, so I set about learning as many types of diamond hitches as I could. I practiced them constantly in my regular Forest Service work. I was interested in the aparejo packsaddle so long used by the U.S. Cavalry. Mr. H.W. Daly, a chief army packer, has written books on that style of pack transportation under the direction of the quartermaster general.

Many times when I worked in areas where diamond hitches were used and someone boasted about their methods and made fun of the way packing was done up where I was raised, I would offer to bet $100 that I could put on twice as many different styles of diamond hitches as any man they could produce. I may well have lost my $100 at some of these times, but I was never challenged.

In working with or helping a packer now, I make it a practice never to give opinions on the methods unless asked for. Any good packer is proud of his work and his methods. The same goes for horsemanship.

A few friends I had worked with in the Forest Service had started working for the Park Service in Glacier and had suggested that I make the change. I had wearied somewhat of the long periods spent in the outlying stations so far from the sort of activities I enjoyed and had already been giving a thought to a change. The St. Joe Forest had written and were offering me a "main line" packing job, the most desirable for a packer because of few camp moves and less cargoing. Jake Williams, head of the Forest Service Remount Depot, had also written and offered me a job.

I thought much about the two offers. Both were choice jobs for those times, as unemployment in the nation was at an all-time high, but decided to talk to George N. "Tiny" Paige, the Glacier Park Fire Chief, before deciding on either. It was on Washington's birthday that I went from Kalispell to Belton on the train. There was five feet of snow as I walked from Belton over to the Park Headquarters. Mr. Paige gave me a run-down on the job he had—it would be a sort of head packer job in the fire control division. I would have just two packers working for me, and I would be a working boss. He kept reminding me of the good men who had already applied for this job and made it sound as though I would have to be extremely lucky to be chosen.

I knew that he had complete information on my experience and qualifications, supplied by those who knew me, some of whom were his right-hand men. He said it would be some time before he would decide which of us to select and would let me know in due time. I didn't feel that it would be very fair to the two Forest Service offers to keep them waiting that long, so as I was leaving, and he shook hands with me, I said, "If you haven't decided in favor of me for the job within two weeks, just tear up my application and forget about me—that is as long as I can wait." He answered me by saying in his southern accent, "You can consider the job yours right now."

As I was growing up, our family always had a few outings to Glacier Park, the place that I was to work off and on for most of the years from

1932 into the 1980s. At first there was no road beyond Apgar at the foot of Lake McDonald. As the road building progressed up along the lake and beyond, so also did our picnic dinner sites. The first time I went to Avalanche Creek, my brother, Tom, and a neighbor boy, Clayton Patterson, and I hiked two miles beyond the road's end to get there. We then hiked on up to Avalanche Lake. In our stops at Apgar, we would often see Charles Russell, who maintained his summer studio there.

One of the highlights of the spring of 1932 in Tiny Paige's department, for which I worked, was a forest firefighting school and conference held at Fish Creek Campground. A regular fire camp was set up, and all fire personnel—such as dispatchers, fire guards, packers, lookout men and all of the park rangers—were in attendance. I remember that all the rangers except Andy Fleutsch, the Kintla Lake ranger, were always in full uniform and spotlessly groomed. The fire guards and lookout men wore uniform trousers, shirts, ties and hats. Fleutsch was also well dressed in his own way, in fairly new Filson "tin" pants and cruiser jacket, topped by a fiery red handlebar mustache and white cowboy hat.

At that time the other rangers were Chief Ranger Earl Dissmore and Assistant Chief Charlie Croghan, West, Park Headquarters. Hugh Peyton, a new ranger, was assigned to the fire division as dispatcher. Glenn Dyer was fire guard at Kintla; Hugh Buchanan, Polebridge; Channing Howell, Flathead Ranger Station (then called North Fork); Ray Newberry, Lake McDonald; Frank Guardipee, Nyack (his fire guard was Fred Benson); and Ben Miller, Paola and Walton, with Jim Croymans as fire guard.

Vern Hedman was fire guard at Fielding, and Hilbert Krause was the ranger at Lubec. Tom Whitcraft was assistant chief ranger, East, at East Glacier Park, with Don Barnum as fire guard. Clyde Fauley was the ranger at Two Medicine; Harry Doust was the ranger at Cut Bank; and Elmer Fladmark was at St. Mary, with Oscar Dick as fire guard. At Sun Camp, Art Best was the ranger and Allen Cook the fire guard. Cy Harkins was the ranger at Many Glacier, with Burt Edwards as fire guard. Elmer Ness was at Belly River and Lou Hanson was at Waterton. The latter two, along with Fleutsch, were single men.

It was a good fire school, well conducted, and every phase of fire control was covered, from getting to the tiny lightning fire while it was still tiny to controlling the one-thousand-acre "project" fires. They were a good bunch of fellows, and I got acquainted with one and all. I was pleased to have every ranger, in turn during the four days, single me out and talk about the subject nearest their hearts. Some asked about the country I had worked

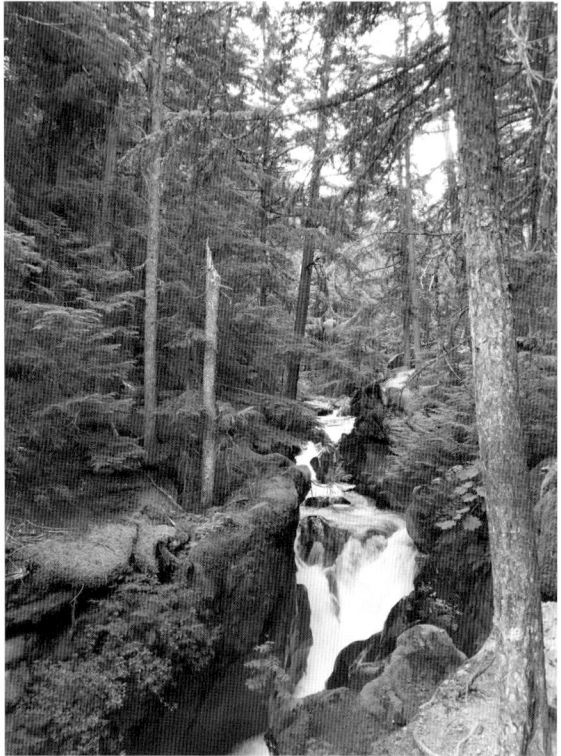

*Right*: The cascades on lower Avalanche Creek near where it flows into McDonald Creek upriver from Lake McDonald. *W.P. Yenne.*

*Below*: The author's great-grandson, Cash Bolos, and his son, W.P. Yenne, take a break after hiking into Avalanche Lake.

in, as some had worked in the same areas. Others were interested in my reaction to the manner in which some of the big fires I had worked on in Montana and Idaho had been handled. Most, however, asked me countless questions about the handling of livestock and about transporting various items by pack animal in the backcountry.

All rangers were required to furnish horses. Glacier is a million-acre wilderness with some of the most mountainous terrain in the world, and these men were responsible for administering and protecting it.

The class sessions were held at Apgar in a large building formerly known as "Gold's Bungalow." It had been recently purchased from its private owner by the National Park Service. This building was later moved to Park Headquarters and is now known as the Conference Training Hall.

In 1934, President Franklin D. Roosevelt visited Glacier, and I was the youngest guard the Park appointed to guard the motorcade as it traveled up to Logan Pass on the Going-to-the-Sun Road. I was in charge of the spur road at the head of Lake McDonald that led into what was then the McDonald Ranger Station, where Ray Newberry was the park ranger. At that time, two U.S. senators from Montana, Burton K. Wheeler and Tom Walsh, both had homes there.

When the open-top red buses with the president's party came by, my job was to not let anyone past a certain point, which was about thirty feet from the edge of the road. There were Secret Service men everywhere, but this part of the job they turned over to me. When onlookers could see the first bus coming down the road, they started to crowd up. I tried to be tough, but Mrs. Wheeler and the older Wheeler children all knew me because they had a couple of saddle horse and I had nail shoes on them and that sort of thing, so they didn't take me very seriously and crowded up a little more.

The bus ahead of the one with President Roosevelt carried Senator Wheeler and Eleanor Roosevelt. When it got even with us, the youngest Wheeler girl shouted, "Hi, Daddy," and I saw Mrs. Roosevelt turn and say something to Senator Wheeler. Then she leaned forward and said something to the driver, who stopped and Mrs. Roosevelt opened the door of the bus.

As Eleanor motioned for the girl to come, I knew I'd been defeated, so I followed her up to the bus and lifted her up onto the high running board as Eleanor reached down. As I tell this story, I like to add that "the one time in my life I had a chance to be famous, I fumbled the ball."

[Editor's note: In 1963, nearly three decades later, Glacier's senior leaders were notified confidentially by the Interior Department that President John F. Kennedy planned to visit Glacier in the summer of 1964 and wished to make a backcountry trail ride. By this time, W.J. Yenne was supervisor of backcountry trails in Glacier and the man who routinely escorted visiting dignitaries and government officials on trail rides. As he would be the one who would lead Kennedy's party, Yenne was one of very few people briefed on these plans. It was also understood that earlier in the year he would also escort a Secret Service detail that would evaluate various possible routes. The planning process was suspended when Kennedy was assassinated on November 22, 1963. As of the publication of this edition of this book more than half a century later, no sitting president has ever been on Glacier's backcountry trails and Roosevelt is the only president to have traveled the Going-to-the-Sun Road.]

Working in Glacier National Park proved to be a drastic change from that of the National Forests. Here I was in daily contact with many people. At Park Headquarters it was like living in a small town, and across the river was the village of Belton. Two miles to the north at the foot of Lake McDonald was Apgar Village. There were changes in the scenery of that area however. The fire of 1929 had burned the Apgar Range to the west and the Belton Hills to the east, leaving only scorched landscape. The beautiful western red cedar trees that had bordered that two-mile road between these two hamlets were destroyed. Upriver, on the north side of US Highway 2 and the Middle Fork of the Flathead, was the same, and except for small brush that has grown since, it remains that way today. As spring each year is approaching, people come in droves to park along the road and look across the river at the elk and deer that come there to browse.

Most of the previous residents still remained, although many had been obliged to rebuild their homes. Charles M. Russell had passed away in 1926, but his wife, Nancy, came every summer to their cottage on Lake McDonald. I soon made friends with young Ace Powell, later a famous artist in his own right who, as a lad not yet in his teens, had been given many pointers by Russell to help his natural talent.

I had a new off-white Stetson hat, and Ace had painted on the left side of the crown in color, a saddled horse. This became a popular fad that summer among the Bar-X-Six guides. Ace made many a dollar decorating western hats.

George N. "Tiny" Paige, the Fire Chief, hired twenty horses from Bob Vinson, a rancher at Big Arm on Flathead Lake. Along with his son, George,

Lake McDonald in April, with the mountains still partially covered with snow. From left to right, the most prominent peaks are Stanton Mountain, Mount Cannon, Mount Brown and Edwards Mountain. *W.P. Yenne.*

one of the packers I supervised, I drove them from Big Arm to Belton, stopping overnight at my parents' place near Creston.

One time when there was a forest fire at Akakala Lake, over Numa Ridge from Bowman Lake, George and I left Park Headquarters at dark and trailed our two-pack strings of horses to the base camp all in total darkness, a distance of thirty miles.

I was interested in seeing as much of this beautiful country as I could. The workload after my four years with the Forest Service, with its long miles, heavy loads and some ornery stock, was like a vacation for me. At times "Tiny" Paige and his assistant, Hugh Peyton, fire dispatcher, used to wonder at my making many of the harder trips instead of sending the men I supervised. Every trip was a pleasure for me.

From the Kintla and Kishenehn sectors, and as far up the Boulder Pass Trail as the Alpine Larch grove and southward, I had the chance to visit every drainage and reach the tops of most of the mountain passes. The long drainages with their large creeks, which would be called "rivers" almost any other place, fed into such beautiful lakes as Upper Kintla Lake, Bowman, Quartz and Upper Quartz, Grace, Logging, Trout, Arrow, Evangeline, Harrison and Ole. Of course, all of the fire lookouts on the west side of the Continental Divide were being serviced by the three of us, so I had many a visit to each of them.

In the late spring, however, there had been a few days in which it appeared that I would end my Park Service career before it had started. I had received letters a couple more times from both the St. Joe Forest and the Forest Service Remount Depot renewing their offers of their best-paying jobs. It had become evident to me that even though my present wages were much higher than their offers, I was being charged by the month for both meals and quarters. I was paying for many meals I never had a chance to eat and was sleeping outdoors a great deal of the time while paying for a bunkhouse room. Consequently, my pay was actually less. Dollars were important to me, more so than the comforts, so I went to Paige and Peyton and gave them two weeks' notice that I had decided to take a Forest Service job. I also told them that if they found a replacement for me sooner than two weeks, I would leave when he arrived. They argued that the wages I was being paid were higher, but I reminded them that the Forest Service gave board and room. I said, "Everything except Kodak film and toothpaste."

The man who was head packer for Charles Randels, the chief engineer, Cliff Hinkley, was from the Coeur d'Alene–Clearwater country in Idaho and had packed for the Forest Service with some of the men I had competed with in the packer's contest. He and I had become very good friends and on Saturday nights had gone to dances together with our dates. The following Saturday evening, when I told him that I planned to leave, he really hit the ceiling. He said that he had just got his degree from the University of Washington in civil engineering and that the next year would not be connected with packing but would be in engineering. He told me that he and Mr. Randels had discussed me as being his successor. He said that Mr. Randels had planned to offer me employment into the following winter after Paige and the fire division could release me. He also said that my quitting at that time of year would be harmful to my record. He demanded that I go to Paige and Peyton and tell them that I had changed my mind. He convinced me.

I had gone only a short distance from the bunkhouse toward Paige's office when I met Peyton. Before I could say anything, he shouted, "Unpack your damn suitcase. We've got you a 49 cents a day raise." That, added to my present pay, made it better than the other offers.

The author's pack string of lumber loads on the trail in Glacier National Park.

The engineering department, headed by Charles Randels, had several strings of very good mules, all of them owned by Glacier National Park. My packers George Vinson and Fred Huggins and I, as well as the fire guards (smokechasers) and rangers, used horses entirely.

One day Fred Huggins and I were crossing the Middle Fork River at Nyack thirteen miles upriver from Park Headquarters. With us was Happy Froh, the Upper Nyack fire guard. High water was nearly over, and at that point in the river a ten-foot-deep hole had been washed in the riverbed.

Huggins and Froh had been there the previous day and knew of it. I was riding a short-legged Vinson horse named Comet. Both of those fellows enjoyed a practical joke. We were riding abreast. They chose their route carefully, and as we approached the hole, they distracted me by pretending to point out something on the far shore, or a mountainside, and crowded Comet into the hole. He did not swim a stroke—guess he didn't have time to think of it. I remember seeing the tips of his ears go out of sight, and then he just walked across the bottom of the hole and up the other side. When his head got above the water, he seemed to look where he was and then blew the water out of his nostrils.

As with the Forest Service, our entertainment when out in camps, and also at the Headquarters, consisted of a lot of horseshoe pitching, wrestling, boxing, wrist wrestling and foot racing. At Headquarters and over at Belton we had a lot of foot racing, especially on the cinder depot platform, which was about one hundred yards long. George Vinson never gave up trying to outrun me. He seemed to think that eventually he would make it. When we would be walking along, he would suddenly start to run and shout back, "I'll beat you to the warehouse, the corral, the bunkhouse or whatever." If there was enough distance remaining, I could always pass him.

There was a truck driver who claimed to be a sprinter and challenged me to a race on the Fourth of July for a five-dollar bet. I had never seen him run but figured I could beat him, so gave my five to the stakeholder. One day when George Vinson was doing some chores, they had given him a CCC lad to help him. This boy, about eighteen, was a freckled, dark-haired youth about five-foot-eleven in height. He was wearing safety toe miners' shoes, which were seldom seen in that area. George called me aside and asked if he could put up five dollars on this boy and have him run against Cox, the truck driver, and me on the Fourth. I knew that as scarce as money was, George had to have a good reason for putting five dollars' worth of confidence in this fellow, so I stalled, saying I'd have to get Cox's permission before I could answer him.

At noon in the mess hall, this lad was sitting down the long table about six or eight feet from me, and a seasonal ranger from the checking station was sitting alongside him was talking to him. I couldn't hear what they were saying but did hear the ranger say, "The two-twenty." I knew that remark alluded to the sprinting distance, so my suspicions grew a little stronger. It didn't take long to find out that that lad was Bob O'Malley from Butte High School. He had just set new state high school records in both the 100- and the 220-yard dashes that were to stand for twenty-eight years before they were broken by Larry Questad from Livingston High. Questad later went to Stanford University at Palo Alto, California, on an athletic scholarship, and I read in the newspapers at least a dozen times that he had won one or both of the sprints at major college track meets. His times in winning at these college meets were nearly always the same as those he made in breaking Bob O'Malley's twenty-eight-year-old high school records. In fact, in the 100, his time was consistently 9.6, the same as he made at Missoula that day.

The author leading a pack string and riding Dude on the steep section of the trail to Sperry Chalet from Lake McDonald in 1933.

At the 1968 Olympics at Mexico City, Larry Questad qualified for the finals in the 200-meter dash. The winner of this race, Tommy Smith, won it in the unbelievable and world record time of 19.8. He and John Carlos, also from the USA, who finished third, made some sort of fame, or infamy, when they held their black-gloved fists aloft on the victors' stand when their medals were presented. Questad did not place, but he did not finish last either; he finished ahead of M. Fray of Jamaica and J. Eigenherr of West Germany, but just being in the finals in that kind of competition had to be something for a Livingston, Montana boy. I'm not saying that all this connects me in any way with the Olympics, but you can see that I subtly tried to make it look that way.

An incident I shall always remember happened east of Logan Pass on the old Logan Pass Trail. I had gone over Gunsight Pass from Lake McDonald and had stayed overnight at Mount Reynolds Lookout, where Lee Buschue and his wife were the lookouts. Charles Peterson, head warehouseman, had accompanied me. The next day, we inventoried the lookout station and moved Buschue's effects down to the road at Sun Camp. That night still stands out clearly in my mind—sitting on the catwalk of the Mount Reynolds Lookout with Lee and Margaret Buschue and Charlie, watching three construction companies working on the Going-to-the-Sun Road, a short airline distance away across the deep valley. These companies included A.R. Douglas Company, which built more road in Glacier than any other and was said to be the only one to have ever really made money at it; Guthrie and Colonial were the other two. As we visited, we could see their lights, watch and hear the equipment working and actually, on a few occasions, when there was a quiet moment, hear men talking. This road was opened to the public on July 15 the next year.

The incident I mentioned happened after we left Sun Camp and were just east of being directly above the east side tunnel of the new road. My caboose horse was a very wild animal named Sailor. Charles was riding just ahead of me so we could visit as we rode along. We met a couple of hikers at this point, both loaded down with camera equipment. Each had nearly as many straps around his neck as there were on Sailor's packsaddle. At this point the trail was so narrow, and the cliff so precipitous, that there was no way these people could get out of the trail. The usual rule is for hikers to stand on the lower side of the trail when meeting stock, but this was impossible in this instance, so I told them to stand in a small niche on the upper side where a small stream of water was falling into the trail. I had instructed them to stand perfectly quiet, as the trail was narrow, and the cliff down to the road some five hundred feet below was almost sheer.

We eased by the hikers. I was watching every move of the animals behind me. As Sailor got almost opposite them, he suddenly noticed them standing there in that niche, and I swear I think he thought he could actually jump out, make a half circle in the air and land back in the trail. At least it looked that way to me, watching him make that leap like a basketball player making a layup past his opposition. Well, Sailor almost made it…but not quite. When he finally landed, he was hanging in a vertical position by only his two knees, from the extreme outer edge of the trail. His knees were hooked on solid rock, and all of the rest of him was actually hanging out there in thin air!

I stopped breathing for a few seconds, my heart stopped beating and the mechanism that heats my blood shut off completely. I know my blood turned cold in those few seconds as I saw his hind legs hanging so far down that cliff. Then he did something that nothing outside the goat or feline families could possibly do: he brought his hind feet forward, and somehow they hooked on a slight, sturdy projection. He gave a grunt and a heave and the next instant he was standing on all fours, crosswise in the narrow trail.

Fortunately, I had been watching closely and had stopped the animal ahead of Sailor and the other stock in a position that he had a place to land and yet far enough back that there was no interference with his lead rope. Many times, coming from the east on the Going-to-the-Sun Road, I have looked up there as I neared the east side tunnel at this now long unused trail, at the spot where the small stream crosses, and thought of Sailor's great leap. Even then, many years later, a slight chill would run up my back.

As the fire season ended, all of the lookouts had been closed and shuttered against the storms of winter, and most of the small fire-trail crews brought in. Mr. Randels called me to his office and gave me a run-

The author at Lake McDonald in 1933, packing a Rix Six compressor engine block, complete with crankshaft, pistons and connecting rods.

down on his plans for me as soon as I could be released by Tiny Paige. I would be going to the "east side."

Before telling about my work there, I will tell about Charles E. Randels, Glacier's chief engineer. First of all, he was an extremely capable engineer. He was a stern taskmaster. He was an expert at writing justifications to the park superintendent, the regional office, the Washington office of the National Park Service and, finally, but most importantly, the Bureau of the Budget for projects he deemed important, most notably Ptarmigan Tunnel, which I discuss in the following chapter. He always had money for road maintenance, had many thirty-man crews building principal tourist trails throughout the most scenic portions of the Park and bought the best equipment, machinery and livestock available.

W.J. Yenne at the south portal of the Ptarmigan Tunnel in the summer of 1966, with Mount Wilbur in the background.

*Chapter 7*

# THE PTARMIGAN TUNNEL STORY

T he idea for a trail tunnel through the Ptarmigan Wall came from Charles Randels, who was the chief engineer in Glacier in the late 1920s and early 1930s. As summarized in a 1931 article in *Pacific Builder & Engineer Magazine*, the old Red Gap Trail was a steep and difficult route over Red Cap Pass that connected the Belly River Valley with Many Glacier, the trail hub of the east side of the Park. Mr. Randels had the idea for a trail tunnel that would "give tourists more marvelous scenery, horses a better chance and the Park an additional improvement." He proposed his idea to Superintendent J. Ross Eakin, who shared it with Chief Engineer Frank A. Kittridge of the National Park Service San Francisco office. Both men approved the plan for a tunnel.

The work was done in less than two months during the summer of 1930. Crews worked from both sides with a Rix Six compressor running four jackhammers on each side. When the job was done, the tunnel was 183 feet long and 9 feet tall, purposely designed to permit people on horseback to pass though easily.

In later years, I recall packing these same compressors, each of which weighed 2,700 pounds, complete with tanks. Several times in moving a thirty-man trail camp, I packed a complete compressor in one trip on ten mules. When mechanics would assemble them out in the mountains, it was difficult for them to get the bearings onto the crankshaft the way they would like. Often, because of this, bearings would burn out more quickly. I perfected a method of packing them on top of a packsaddle in one piece, like I had done many times in transporting large six-hole kitchen ranges. This made it possible for the mechanics to assemble it in the shop.

*Left*: Glacier National Park chief engineer Charles E. Randels (*left*) with George Reed, the assistant engineer, at Ptarmigan Tunnel in 1932.

*Below*: The first horses through the Ptarmigan Tunnel were Sunday and Sid. Mrs. C.E. Randels is on Sid.

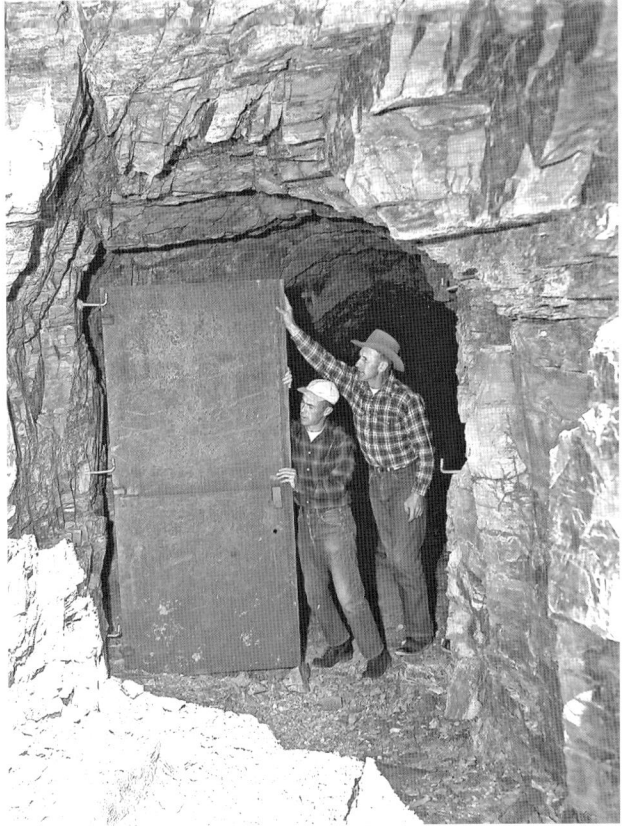

The author and
Ranger Jim Godbolt
inspecting one of
the steel doors of the
Ptarmigan Tunnel in
September 1960 prior
to sealing the tunnel
for the winter.

As I recall, Charles Randels's favorite saddle horse was a beautiful black named Dude, who continued to be a very good trail horse in Glacier until he was twenty-five years old. I rode him myself many times through the years. Mrs. Randels was responsible for her husband having Dude. She loved horses and was skillful in handling and caring for them. She was a very good rider and knew the selection of horses for purchasing. A story was told to me many times by Mr. Randels about Dude crossing one of Glacier's raging streams during high water on a narrow foot-log that had been hewn flat on the top side. Mr. Randels insisted that Dude had done it, and the three-man trail crew who also claimed to have seen it swore that it was true.

Through the years after Charles Randels left Glacier, he and his wife proved to be very good pen pals. After he passed away, Mrs. Randels continued to write to me occasionally. In 1966, she decided that I was the one to have all of Charles's records and articles pertaining to the construction of the Ptarmigan Tunnel. Many years before, at a National

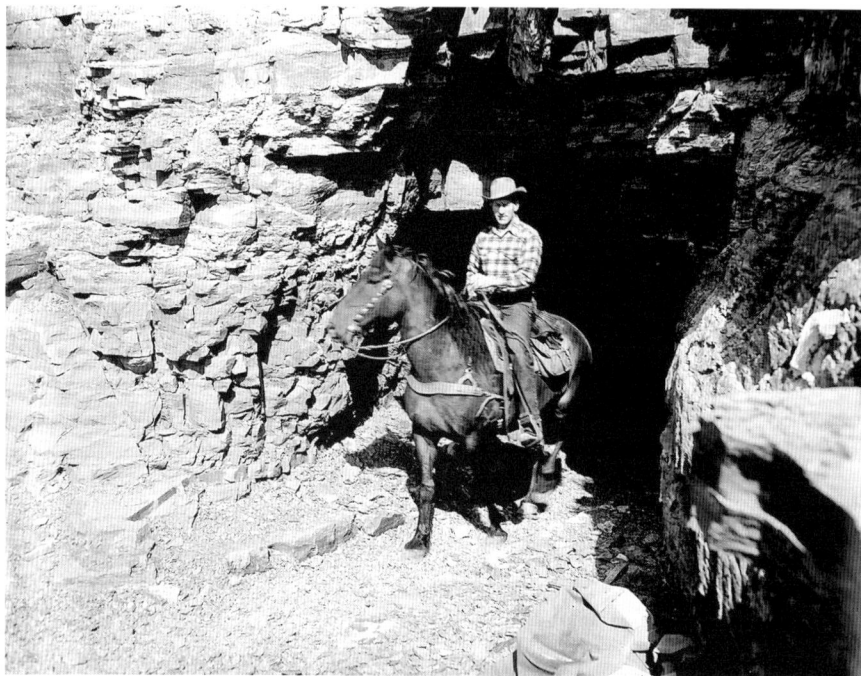

The author exiting the Ptarmigan Tunnel on a 1966 inspection trip.

Bison Range at Moise, Montana, Charles had been allowed to shoot a buffalo bull in a herd reduction. From the hide he had a Gladstone suitcase made. The suitcase was lined with tanned buckskin from a deer he had killed. Mrs. Randels put all of the photos, records, clippings, etc., in that Gladstone and sent it to me.

The Ptarmigan Tunnel was one of his fondest dreams and projects. To this day, it is one of the foremost man-made wonders in the entire National Park System. All who understand construction, or even those who do not but have an eye for architectural beauty, always are in awe as they come upon it. During my years in Glacier, I have been fortunate to be chosen to guide the parties of park officials and officials from the regional and Washington offices, as well as distinguished guests of theirs, on the backcountry pack trips. It was always my duty to plan the itinerary, and I always, if allowed, included the trail to the Ptarmigan Tunnel.

# Ptarmigan Wall Tunnel Completed In Glacier National Park

By H. Geiger

**C.** E. RANDELS, Park Engineer of Glacier National Park and his assistant engineer, G. W. Reed, made final inspection of Ptarmigan Wall tunnel when the first saddle horses were ridden through its portals last fall. This tunnel is 183' long, nine feet high and has parking space at each portal, made safe by rock guard walls designed by Landscape Engineer E. O. Davidson.

The old Red Gap trail was a torturously steep and rocky way over which horses had strained and sweated with packs and people for many years. One day Mr. Randels conceived the idea of a trail tunnel which would give tourists more marvelous scenery, horses a better chance and the park an additional improvement. He took his idea and his estimate to the Superintendent of Glacier National Park, J. Ross Eakin, who gave the project his approval and in turn gained the approval of Chief Engineer Frank A. Kittridge of the San Francisco office for National Park Service. This tourist trail starts from Many Glaciers Hotel, passes up Wilbur creek with its gorge at Ptarmigan falls and around Ptarmigan lake up a 15% grade to the south portal of the tunnel. Dismounting, the riders see a wonderful picture of many peaks, namely Mt. Wilbur, Mt. Grinnel, Piegan and Going-to-the-Sun mountains. Riding through the tunnel is made safe by low rock walls the length of the tunnel so horses must walk the center line and will not be able to get near the jagged rocks.

From the north portal the trail comes down the side of a bright red mountain with lovely Lake Elizabeth below. It is 9 miles on to Crosley Lake for the night. The trail passes many water falls of which Dawn Mist is one of the

C. E. Randels, Park Engineer, Glacier National Park, and G. W. Reed, assistant engineer, on Ptarmigan Wall where the new trail tunnel was completed.

highest in the park and considered by many the most spectacular. Two Rix air compressors were used on this trail and tunnel and they as well as supplies and powder were packed seven miles up the mountain by Park Service mules. Forty-five boxes of 40% powder and 12 boxes of 60% were used. The job took two months and the tunnel cost $3100, with rock wall work paid extra.

This article about the building of the Ptarmigan Tunnel appeared in the May 2, 1931 issue of *Pacific Builder & Engineer Magazine*.

Triple Divide Peak towers over the pass of the same name where riders are stopped for lunch. Located at the intersection of the Continental Divide and the Hudson Bay Divide on what was once a popular Bar-X-Six route, this location marks the only geographic point in North America with drainage into three oceans. Water from a canteen spilled here can theoretically drain into the Atlantic via tributary streams of the Missouri River, the Pacific via the Columbia River and the Arctic via the Saskatchewan River and Hudson Bay.

## Chapter 8

# THE BAR-X-SIX STORY

The horse concession in Glacier National Park in the 1930s was a gigantic operation. Newspaper articles from big eastern papers and stories in leading magazines proclaimed it the world's largest dude ranch, with hundreds of miles of scenic trails and tent camps at Red Eagle and Crosley Lakes and at Fifty Mountain. The concession operated the Goathaunt Chalets on Waterton Lake in addition to horse camps at Lake McDonald, East Glacier Park, Two Medicine, Cut Bank, Sun Camp and Many Glacier.

It is unlikely that any saddle horse operation anywhere ever came close to equaling it. At Many Glacier alone, three hundred horses were used, and there were times that even then they ran so short of horses and guides that the blacksmith would put a saddle on the draft horse used to haul wood for heating the boilers and fill in as a guide to take a party to Iceberg or Ptarmigan Lakes. I might add that this particular work horse was a mighty good mount under the saddle, as I had occasion to meet him on the trails a few times. Altogether, the Park Saddle Horse Company, better known by its brand as the Bar-X-Six, had well over one thousand head of horses and employed over 125 people.

The Glacier Park Hotel Company, the Park's prime concessionaire, owned and operated a four-hundred-room hotel at Many Glacier and the three-hundred-room Glacier Park Lodge at East Glacier Park (originally Midvale). They operated the Lake McDonald Hotel, then still referred to as the Lewis Hotel and now called the Lake McDonald Lodge, which the

The Park Saddle Horse Company (Bar-X-Six) camp at Crossley (later Cosley) Lake in 1937.

National Park Service had recently purchased from John Lewis. The hotel company also owned and operated chalets at Two Medicine, Cut Bank Creek, St. Mary, West Glacier (then Belton), the huge chalet complex at Sun Point and the two mountain chalets, Sperry and Granite Park, which were reached only by trail. Since a large percentage of the Park's visitors arrived by rail, the bus operation, run by Howard Hayes, was also a very large concession. They operated some thirty red buses, made by the White Motor Company, with tops that could be put down in fair weather, affording the passengers a panoramic view of Glacier's marvelous scenery. Glacier and Waterton had joined to create the Waterton-Glacier International Peace Park, and the Prince of Wales Hotel at Waterton, Alberta, was a part of Glacier's overall hotel operation.

The principal trail trips were the North and South Circles, the former including Many Glacier, Swiftcurrent Pass, Granite Park, Fifty Mountain, Goathaunt Camp at Waterton Lake, Stoney Indian Pass, Crosley Lake Camp, Ptarmigan Pass and the Ptarmigan Tunnel, thence back to Many

Glacier. The South Circle includes Lake McDonald, Sperry Glacier and Chalet, Lake Ellen Wilson, Gunsight Pass and Lake, Sun Camp, Piegan Pass, Many Glacier, Swiftcurrent Pass, Granite Park and down McDonald Creek to Lake McDonald again. These trips, of course, were also made in reverse. A shorter trip, called "The Triangle," included McDonald, Sun Point and Granite Park via the Logan Pass Trail and back to Lake McDonald. Another version included Many Glacier, Sun Camp (now just Sun Point) and Granite Park.

Another very popular trip was the "Inside." It ran between Sun Camp or Many Glacier and East Glacier Park and took in Red Eagle Lake and Triple Divide Pass. To the west of Triple Divide Pass is a small peak of the same name, which is a promontory of Norris Mountain, from which flows Hudson Bay Creek, Atlantic and Pacific Creeks. The headwaters of the three actually are within feet of one another, and each eventually flows into the body of water for which it is named. At this point, the Hudson Bay Divide connects with the Continental Divide. With Hudson Bay ultimately draining into the Arctic Ocean, this is the only point in North America with drainage into three oceans!

The trail descends past Medicine Grizzly Lake, with the overnight stop at Cut Bank Chalets. From there the trail passes beautiful Morning Star Lake, Pitamakin Lake and a small unnamed lake, which was commonly called "Jonah's Bowl" in those days. There were camping trips that lasted a full month, and the campers—as well as those who stayed at the hotels, chalets and the Bar-X-Six Saddle Horse Company's camps—always had good trout fishing near at hand.

To tell the story of the Park Saddle Horse Company and its operation in Glacier National Park, one had best go back to tell of the independent operators, or outfitters, who first took horse parties into the Park. Thomas Dawson was one of the very earliest of these operators and may well have been the first to take parties into the Park from the Midvale area. This is the area surrounding East Glacier Park. Dawson Pass was named for him, and he is known to have taken hunting parties into what is now Glacier National Park before it was made a park in 1910.

Tom and Isabelle Dawson had a daughter, Helene. From 1914 to 1917 Helene attended high school in Great Falls with Sidney Brewster, the daughter of Bill Brewster, who is mentioned here below. Helene Dawson was married to George Edkins, and for many years they operated the main general store in East Glacier Park. Since George's death, and all throughout the 1970s, Helene has operated Helene's giftshop there.

This 1925 illustration by Joseph Scheuerle shows a Park Saddle Horse Company guide and some park visitors enjoying a ride. Note the Bar-X-Six brand ("-X6") on each of the horses.

George Jennings came to Midvale (now East Glacier) in 1908. He "proved up" on a homestead fourteen miles southeast of Midvale in 1910. He was Louis Hill's personal guide all of the time Louis was in Glacier. George's widow, Betsy, is still in contact with the Louis Hill family. She makes her home in Kalispell, Montana. Both the towns of Midvale and Belton were on the mainline of the Great Northern Railway. Louis Hill was the son of the Great Northern's founder, James J. Hill.

After Glacier became a park in 1910, and even before, there were several outfitters operating out of Belton and Apgar on the west side of the Park. The best known of these were Ski Keckler, Joe Rogers, Frank Higgins, Faldy Neitzling and Ernie LaNeau. In 1912, Neitzling and LaNeau packed the material to Gunsight Lake for the construction of the chalet there. Ed Neitzling, Faldy's younger brother, just a school boy when he helped them, has told me of packing in the massive kitchen range stripped of all removable parts and mounted on a travois. Before the Gunsight Chalet was completed, an avalanche off Fusillade Mountain demolished it and swept it into Gunsight Lake.

Jack Weightman operated a livery stable business at Belton and Apgar and often worked in cooperation with the outfitters mentioned here. Belton had its name changed to West Glacier on October 1, 1949. Coincidentally, my son, William P. Yenne, was born that exact day at Grand Canyon Village in Arizona. This was when I was working at Grand Canyon National Park (see chapter 11). We later moved back to Glacier, and he grew up across the Middle Fork of the Flathead River from West Glacier and attended primary school there.

During this period, there was operating out of Banff, Alberta, a company known as the Brewster Transportation Company. It consisted of four of the Brewster brothers: Jim, Bill, George and Fred. There was also a younger brother, Pat, not in the company. At this writing, Pat is the only one of the brothers still alive.

About 1915 three of the brothers, Bill, George and Fred, sold their interest in the Banff enterprise to their brother Jim and started an operation in Glacier, also called Brewster Transportation. According to available information, they induced the National Park Service to grant them a concession for all horse operations within the Park. Some of the operators aforementioned have told me that they were, in a sense, "run out," to use their words.

During the next two or three years, the Brewsters enlarged their operation in Glacier, adding to the number of horses and taking out more and larger parties. George Brewster ran the operation at Lake McDonald, Fred at Many Glacier and Bill at Midvale or East Glacier Park. Bill had two grown sons, Jack and Claude. The latter married Ruth Dorrington, the daughter of Bill Dorrington, a park ranger. His daughter, Sidney, attended high school in Great Falls with Helene Dawson Edkins.

In 1917, the Brewster brothers sold out their operation to Wilbur N. Noffsinger and went back to Banff to work for their brother Jim, who had bought out their interests there. After that, all three continued to work for Jim, who was proving to be a very shrewd businessman. During the late 1970s in Santa Cruz, California, I became well acquainted with Jim Brewster's wife, Adele, who spends three or more months in Santa Cruz each winter, though she still makes her permanent home in Banff.

An interesting sidelight concerns a schoolmate in Banff of Adele and her sister, Kina, a good friend of mine named Harry Knight of Fowler, Colorado. He once was very prominent in big-time rodeo and was married to Ruth Mix, the daughter of Tom Mix, the western movie star. In 1940, Harry and Ruth were living in Arizona. On October 12, 1940, Tom Mix was on his way to visit them driving his custom-built, yellow Cord convertible. There was some construction going on at a wash that now bears Tom Mix's name, and it was there that he crashed into the wash and was killed. Later, Harry Knight was, for many years, a partner of Gene

A group of Bar-X-Six guides and their clients during a lunch stop near Piegan Pass on the Continental Divide between the St. Mary and Swiftcurrent Valleys in June 1932 at the time the author was working in the park. Note the ranger seated at the left. *National Park Service.*

Autry in the rodeo production business. Harry told me of having worked for Jim Brewster in Banff when in his teens. Adele Brewster affirmed this in our later conversations in Santa Cruz.

Before leaving Midvale, Bill Brewster sold his ranch there to George Jennings, who owned and operated this ranch until 1942, when he sold it to Tex and Carmella Hughes. Tex and his brother, Ves, had worked for Jennings on the ranch. In 1936, at the time of the Heavens Peak Fire, the Hughes brothers ran pack strings in the Many Glacier area, supplying fire camps and packing pumps, hose and tools to the firefighters. I was told that they were using Jennings horses, but I am not sure of this. The stock may have been their own.

On the west side of Glacier, at least two of the operators still remained very active. They were Joe Rogers and Frank Higgins. Some of the others may also have, but I am sure of these two.

During my family's picnic excursions to Lake McDonald, and as far beyond as the road building progress would allow, around 1925 I remember seeing the pack camps from which Rogers, Higgins, Dallas Disbrow and other operators were supplying the road building contractor. As I recall, Mr. A.R. Douglas was the principal contractor.

With the coming of fall snows on the Continental Divide and the closing down of road building, the abovementioned operators would move their stock to Coram and would take hunting parties up the South Fork of the Flathead River.

Ed Neitzling worked at this time for Frank Higgins and in the teens and early '20s packed and guided Charles M. Russell's hunting parties. In Russell's book, *Good Medicine*, there are copies of letters written to Ed.

By the time the Brewsters sold out their operation to Noffsinger (about 1917), more trails were being built in the Park. De Wanser had worked for Joe Rogers in 1916 and had stayed at Apgar with Weightmans, taking horses from there to the head of Lake McDonald.

The North Circle camps were started in 1924. They continued until 1941. De Wanser tells of being a camping guide for Noffsinger in 1919, 1921, 1922 and 1923. The latter two years he was at Two Medicine and operated the horse camp there where Mrs. Wanser cooked for the men. Freight for the Crossley Lake camp was hauled in by wagon from BB Flats in Alberta. Crossley Lake and Ridge were named for an early day engineer (this I was told by many old-timers), but the name was later changed to honor a former forest ranger turned trapper and poacher, Joe Cosley.

Some of the supplies for Goathaunt Chalet, a part of the Noffsinger North Circle operation, were brought in by boat from Waterton Townsite in Alberta. Most, however, were packed all the way from Many Glacier by the North Circle Pack Strings, which also supplied Fifty Mountain Camp and Granite Park Chalet. Supplies that reached Cosley Lake Camp by pack train from Many Glacier came by way of Red Gap Pass until the fall of 1931, when the trail past Ptarmigan Lake and through Ptarmigan Tunnel was made passable.

All through the 1920s, the operation grew by leaps and bounds. When Wilbur Noffsinger died in 1924, his son, George Noffsinger, took over. The size of the individual groups was astounding. The Howard Eaton party in 1916 had had 150 horses. From 1932 on through the 1930s, my work took me over all of the trails in the Park, and on the principal tourist trails (called dude trails) I have often met parties with as many as 100 horses.

Noffsinger operated with over 1,000 horses, and some have said that their horse herd numbered over 1,500 in all. Horse breakers were kept busy all through the spring, summer and fall seasons. Although the Arab horse is not considered a good mountain horse because of their size and low (mutton)

The Granite Park Chalet, like its sister chalet at Sperry, was an important overnight stop for Bar-X-Six overnight trips. Both chalets continued to operate after the Park Saddle Horse Company ceased its activities during World War II. *W.P. Yenne.*

withers, those half-Arabian horses raised there on the Bar-X-Six ranch were very good horses for their size. Many were from larger mares and were top-notch mountain horses. The Bar-X-Six was permitted to graze their horses in most areas of the Park. At Many Glacier they were turned out to go up on the ridge toward Kennedy Creek on the slope of Appekunny Mountain and also were allowed to graze along Sherbourne Lake. Every night of the summer there would be at least 300 horses at Many Glacier. When large trail parties were to start from there, or had ended there, the number would exceed 400 head. Some of the men who managed the Many Glacier operation (often called corral bosses) with whom I became acquainted were Bill Gird, Bill Humble, Ross Jordan, John E. Peterson and Roland Tibbetts.

After two Arabian stallions were killed by lightning in the Bar-X-Six barn, George Noffsinger secured two thoroughbred stallions on loan from the U.S. Army Remount. One of the remount stallions, Plenipotentiary, was a half brother of Man o' War, rated by *Sports Illustrated* and the Associated Press as the "outstanding race horse of the century." Both had been sired by Fair Play, a bronky thoroughbred racehorse and multiple stakes winner. Harold Hadfield, a Bar-X-Six horse breaker, worked with Plenipotentiary trying to get him reasonably gentled. I never actually saw him buck that hard, but he always had a hump in his back and the hind end of Hadfield's saddle was always a few inches above the horse's back.

From these two thoroughbred stallions and the good Bar-X-Six mares came a multitude of very good trail horses over the years. A neighboring rancher, Jack Galbraith, was one who also had the services of these stallions. From Plenipotentiary he raised a stallion that sired many of the best cow horses that range had ever seen. Ranchers told me of using some of these horses for roping stock at branding time. Instead of the ropers changing horses during the day as one animal would get tired, with these horses they changed riders and the horse continued on all day.

In the mid-1960s, another rancher in that area, Arthur W. "Doug" Douglas, who had worked all through the 1930s as a Bar-X-Six guide, got a particular colt from a Galbraith stallion, a son of the first one. This Douglas colt was broken to ride when a three-year-old. In his fourth year he got with some half wild horses in the Chief Mountain area and was not corralled the entire year. As a five-year-old, he bucked off every rider that attempted to ride him. Douglas finally hired him out to Hugo Johnson, an outfitter, for a pack horse. There also he proved very intractable, so Douglas sold him to a horse dealer named Eddy Vaughn, who sold him to Buetler Brothers, rodeo producers from Elk City, Oklahoma. In the five years of 1965 through 1969, this horse, named "Descent" by Buetlers, was named champion bucking horse of the year by the top twenty bronc riders of the Professional Rodeo Cowboy Association. In 1970, he was injured in a hauling accident and was out of competition most of the year. However, in 1971 he again won the honor for an unprecedented sixth time.

According to existing records loaned to me by Mrs. Edwina Noffsinger, now making her home at the Bar-X-Six ranch headquarters at Duck Lake, a few miles from Babb, Montana, Noffsinger also purchased many horses from neighboring ranchers. W.R. Logan and Ross Jordan are shown as two of his men who acted as purchasing agents for him. Also he sold some half thoroughbred horses to the U.S. Cavalry. This may have been a clause in the agreement whereby he secured the services of Plenipotentiary.

[Editor's note: According to the Montana Historical Society Research Center, in its heyday, the Park Saddle Horse Company did indeed own at least one thousand horses and served nearly ten thousand tourists annually. Before the opening of the Going-to-the-Sun Road over Logan Pass in 1933, the only way of seeing the most magnificent scenery of the Park was by horseback. When travelers were able to reach the heart of the Park by car, things changed. Then came World War II. In 1942, the National Park Service decided to close all the Park concessions for the duration. Unable to support his large horse herd for an indefinite period, George Noffsinger sold them. The concession was canceled by the National Park Service at his request in 1945. He passed away two years later.]

In addition to bearing the "-X6" brand, the Bar-X-Six horses were also numbered. It is my belief that they numbered them only up to 1,000. There

The author (*left*) and his son, William P. Yenne, at the crest of Gunsight Pass, circa 1965. Going-to-the-Sun Mountain is the prominent peak in the background. Gunsight Lake, where there was once a chalet used by the Bar-X-Six, is visible just to the right of the horse on the right.

may have been some numbered higher than that, but if so, I never saw them. In 1927, Noffsinger started adding a prefix number. That year the foals were numbered A 1 through A 41. 1928 saw 110 colts branded B 1 through B 110. In subsequent years, this numbering system continued as follows:

| | |
|---|---|
| 1929: C 1 through C 75 | 1936: K 1 through K 37 |
| 1930: D 1 through D 29 | 1937: L 1 through L 54 |
| 1931: E 1 through E 58 | 1938: M 1 through M 48 |
| 1932: F 1 through F 49 | 1939: N 1 through N 84 |
| 1933: G 1 through G 33 | 1940: P 1 through P 89 |
| 1934: H 1 through H 50 | 1941: R 1 through R 53 |
| 1935: J 1 through J 54 | 1942: S 1 through S 28 |

*Opposite*: This 1925 advertisement depicts a young park visitor who is experiencing the wonders of Glacier's backcountry while riding a Bar-X-Six saddle horse.

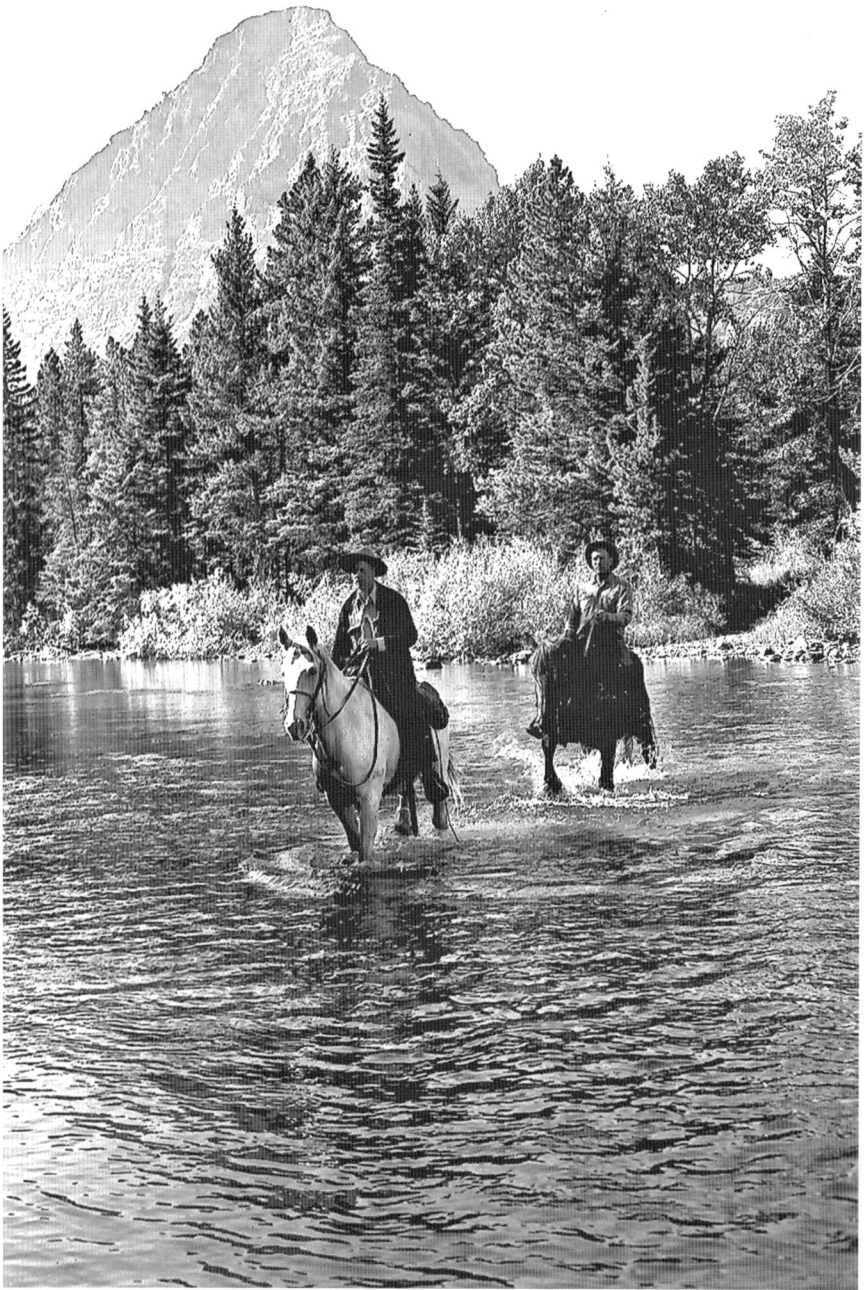

Ranger Joe Heimes and the author (*right*) fording Belly River. In 1929, Heimes achieved notoriety for tracking and capturing the infamous outlaw Joe Cosley in the Belly River Country.

*Chapter 9*

# ON THE EAST SIDE OF GLACIER NATIONAL PARK

I n going to the east side of Glacier Park, Mr. Randels's orders were for me to first go into Two Medicine Valley and move out one of the small crews who had been maintaining the principal, or first class, tourist trails in the area.

There I again saw Ranger Clyde Fauley, whom I had met at the spring conference. He showed me around his area and his ranger station. I met his wife and his small schoolboy sons. After like duties in the Cut Bank and St. Mary Valleys, I ended up at Many Glacier, which was to be my headquarters and principal work center. There I got acquainted with the pack string I was to use. It consisted of nine black mules and a lead pack horse that had been named "Tony" because of his resemblance in color and markings (so the namer thought) to Tom Mix's famous movie horse. Tony had been a member of a bucking horse string but proved to be a faultless lead pack horse. At the head of that string of mules that had not been well halter-broken, he never tightened the leadrope in my hand. My black saddle mount was named Diamond.

A part of my work was to service the mason's camp at Ptarmigan Lake. Adolph Lindgren was the foreman, and they were building all of the masonry parapet walls at the tunnel and along the cliff for a half mile to the north toward Belly River. On the days I packed there, I would leave Many Glacier with a stringload of sand, cement and sometimes groceries. The trail to this point was wide enough to accommodate an Oliver-Cletrac crawler tractor with a thirty-six-inch width. An expert equipment operator named Roy Bengtson operated this tractor and behind it pulled a two-wheeled, rubber-tire trailer.

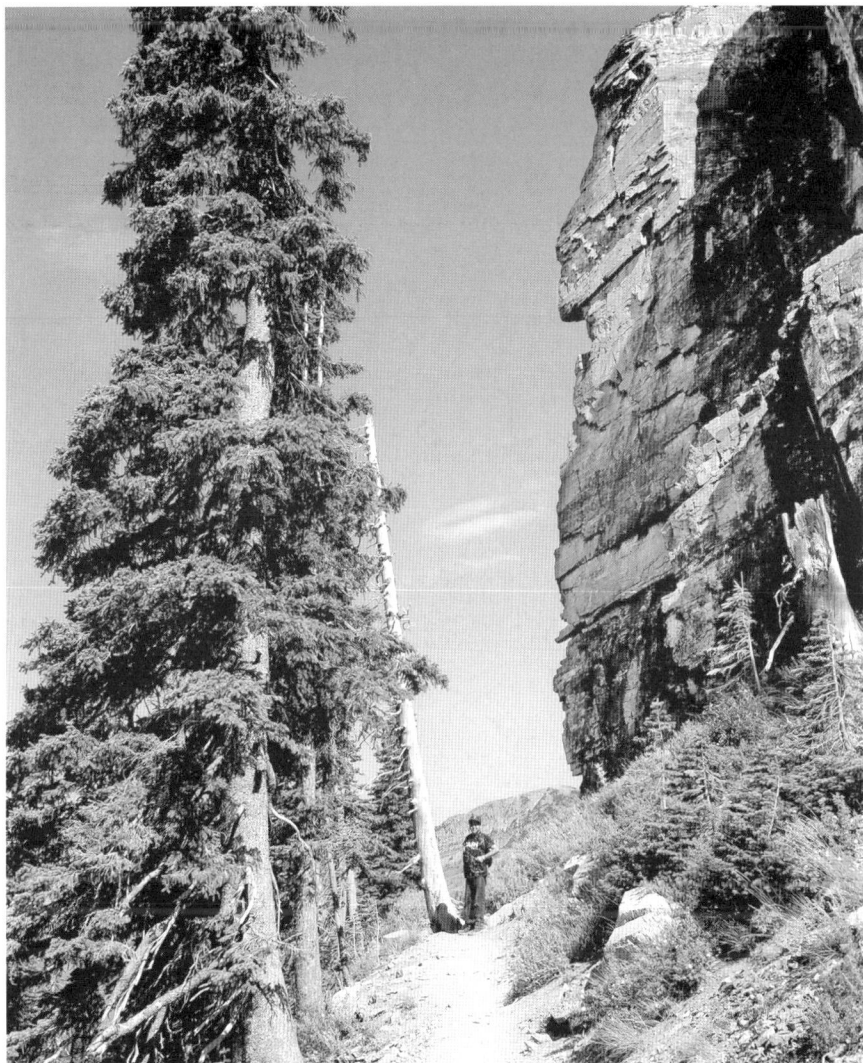

*This page and opposite*: The Highline Trail then and now. The photo on the left of a lone rider, perhaps Charles Randels, was taken about ninety years before the author's great-grandson, Cash Bolos, passed exactly the same spot in 2017. Running between Logan Pass and both Swiftcurrent Pass and Ahern Pass, the Highline Trail is a key trail link between the east and west sides of Glacier. *W.P. Yenne.*

In the box of the trailer he could haul about a yard of sand. Along the sides of the tractor, above the tracks, were planks on which sacks of cement could be loaded.

In leaving Many Glacier with my loaded pack string, I would go directly to, and through, the tunnel and would unload at the locations indicated by Lindgren or his masons. I would then go the more than a mile back to Ptarmigan Lake, where I would reload my string with sand and cement that Bengtson had brought that far. There were no switchbacks on the trail below the lake, so he had clear sailing so long as he stayed on the trail. I would unload my second load and would be back at Many Glacier at about 4:00 p.m. I found that it would take me twenty-five minutes to load my string of ten pack animals. That time varied not a minute day to day. This time included filling the pack boxes with sand.

The other camps that I would pack to between trips to the tunnel were on the other side of the Continental Divide. It was thirty-three miles to Goathaunt Ranger Station at the south end of Waterton Lake. I would go over the Divide at Swiftcurrent Pass, eight miles from Many Glacier. From there it was fourteen miles to Fifty Mountain and another eleven on to Goathaunt. It was an extremely long day for my stock, but this was fall, and all of the summer camps along the way were closed. I would have supplies for construction camps at Pass Creek, Lake Frances and Boundary Creek. The Highline Trail at that time was newly constructed.

On my first trip over this route I had a couple of mule loads that had been cargoed by another packer. He had included a five-gallon tin can of gasoline without protecting it with a wooden box. Along the way, it became kinked by the ropes and started leaking on the mule and was blistering him. I unpacked him twice, poured some out a couple of times and put it in the bottom of the pack and to the outside. It seems that I fought that pack all day, and it was long after dark when I arrived at Goathaunt Ranger Station. I had never been there and began to wonder if I had bypassed it. I had seen five grizzly bears near Fifty Mountain and at dusk in the south end of Waterton Valley had seen a cow moose with twin calves. Suddenly there was a small square of light…the ranger station! Just then, a black bear that had been at the garbage can and had been startled ran through my string. They scattered far and wide in the darkness.

At the mason camp at Ptarmigan Lake, there were ten men, including the foreman and Ed Metzger, the cook. At the camp they had an 1,800-pound draft horse that they hitched to a "skip," a flat steel pan on which they hauled their building rocks from the point where they were quarried to where they were to be used. At camp there was a tent-fly barn for the horse. The manger was about seven feet long, and at night a medium-size black bear that hung around the camp and was fed garbage would sleep in one end of the manger. I have seen times when the horse would whinny for the bear and he would go over where the horse was. The fourteen miles of trail between Granite Park and Fifty Mountain is known as the Highline Trail. It was built in 1928 and 1929 and was another of Mr. Randels's dreams—and his masterpiece.

Before this trail was built, trail parties going from Granite Park Chalet to Fifty Mountain Camp and on to Goathaunt were obliged to go down into the McDonald Valley to Mineral Creek and follow this drainage northward to its head. I will mention at this point that the Bar-X-Six tent camps at Red Eagle Lake, Crossley Lake and Fifty Mountain as overnight or longer stays for their horse parties employed about seven people at each. Sperry and Granite Park Chalets, accessible only by trail, each employed about ten or twelve. Goathaunt camp employed six.

When I made one of my trips to Goathaunt, a small crew of telephone linemen were there. One late fall job to be done was to go to the top of Browns Pass and take the phone line down from the poles to avoid its being broken by winter snow and forming of ice on the wire. Since this was grizzly bear country, it would not be prudent to send one man alone on the eight and a half miles to the pass. That meant that two men would have to go.

The work itself was only a one-man task. There was a saddle in the barn, so I decided to do Bill Stewart, the crew foreman, a favor by lending him my saddle horse and I'd ride Tony to Boundary Creek. I had no doubts as I cinched my Association saddle on Tony that morning. We had become well acquainted, and he had seemed gentle to pack. When I attempted to mount him, however, he was a different horse. He would whirl and plunge, causing me to lose my grip on the rope of the lead mule. After having to dismount a couple of times to retrieve the lead rope, I tied the rope to a tree branch, mounted and plow-reined Tony over and untied it. I then maneuvered Tony up the trail. The farther we went, the better he went, and we reached the Boundary Creek Cabin long before noon.

After lunch I started back, and after a mile or so I came to a steep slide area covered with alders. Halfway across the alder slide, Tony suddenly stiffened and came to a halt. At the far side of the thicket I saw what I first thought to be one of the mules I had left in the corral at Waterton station and which had somehow gotten out of the corral and followed me. Just then, however, it lifted its yard-long head and I saw that it was an extremely large cow moose.

St. Mary Lake, with Wild Goose Island, has long been the signature scenic view from the east side of Glacier National Park. As the author would have told you, as he knew every peak in the park at a glance, the pointed peak in the center is Fusillade Mountain, while prominent on the left are Mahtotopa, Little Chief and Dusty Star Mountains. *W.P. Yenne.*

She took a good long look at us and started walking toward us with head held high, sniffing the air. I could see that she was a foot taller than Tony, and I'm sure he noticed it too, as he was terrified. Tony started backing up, and of course we all were getting tangled up in halter ropes. The trail was too steep for turning around, and I was having my hands full controlling Tony and keeping my short pack string untangled. The moose didn't appear to be on the fight, just curious, but nevertheless none of my shouting and waving seemed to deter her. It only served to frighten Tony all the more.

We must have backed up forty yards before the cow, her curiosity apparently satisfied, turned and went to the far side of the steep slide and then up the hill from the trail. Even with her gone, Tony was still afraid, and he crossed that slide as though walking on eggs.

About this time I had orders to go back to Many Glacier by way of Belly River Ranger Station, where I was to pick up a trail camp that had been vacated. Also, I was to take some building material to the Stoney Indian Pass shelter cabin that was being built. I had met Elmer Ness, the Belly River ranger, that spring at fire and ranger conferences and knew him to be a single man, so figured there would be no problem finding overnight quarters there. There were about fifteen inches of snow on the ground crossing Stoney Indian Pass and about four inches at Belly River.

All buildings were locked, and there was not a human track in the snow anywhere. I cared for my stock, and as there was still no sign of Ness, I again checked all the doors of the ranger station, fire guard cabin and barn/tool shed. It was getting real cold and daylight was fading. I had food with me but no place to cook it, and I didn't like the thought of sleeping outside in my scanty bedroll. Finally, in making another round of the buildings, I pushed against a front window of the ranger station living room and it swung inward—it was hinged and not hooked. I went inside, opened the back door, got some wood and started a fire in the wood range. After I had washed my supper dishes, I found a good magazine and was reading by the light of the Coleman lantern.

As I sat reading, I imagined that I could hear an automobile. While I had never been there before, I knew that it was at least ten miles to any automobile road. Chief Mountain Road would not be built for four more years, and there was just a wagon road down Belly River to Alberta. Sometimes I could hear it—then again I would listen for quite some time and hear nothing. Finally I went to the front door to listen. From there the sound was quite clear, and then suddenly I caught a glimpse through the trees of headlights. As they got nearer I took the lantern and stood in the front doorway as the auto drove up and two people got out and came to the door. I then recognized Elmer Ness.

Now Elmer was a very mild dispositioned man, but when he asked me, "What are you doing here?" he sounded very provoked. I told him who I was and explained why I was there, whereupon he started making me welcome and introduced me to his wife of two days. They had been married in Great Falls.

I quickly made a decision to sleep in the fire cache building, but Elmer said I should sleep upstairs in the ranger station. I felt as low as a caught burglar and didn't want to cause any more inconvenience, so I stuck to my guns and finally persuaded Elmer to unlock the fire cache building. He asked me what time I wanted breakfast, and I told him not to worry about me as I could get my breakfast out there. He insisted and finally won that argument. I left the next morning still feeling less than a foot tall. Elmer and his wife, Margaret, sensed how I felt and often in the years to come kidded me about it. Many times at a social gathering Margaret would say to the people present, "Did I ever tell you about the time Bill Yenne broke into our ranger station?" Then he would laugh and bang me on the shoulder.

About this time I had orders to go to Lake McDonald, where Roy Holbrook, another of Mr. Randels's packers, had a camp, his principal job being to service the thirty-man camp located three-quarters of a mile east of Gunsight Pass. Jim Carey was the foreman of this crew, which were rebuilding the Gunsight Pass Trail from the pass down to Gunsight Lake. Carey was the man who had headed the crew who had pushed Ptarmigan Tunnel through Ptarmigan Wall and built the half mile of very spectacular trail beyond it on the Belly River side. Now with winter approaching, his camp was to be moved out, and a third packer, Walt Teubert, and I had been summoned to help Holbrook pack the camp out.

The crew, before leaving, had taken down all the tents except the 16x24-foot cook tent; had stacked tools, blacksmith forge, steel sharpening equipment, compressor hose, jack hammers, gasoline containers, etc., outside; and had left groceries and bedding in the cook tent.

As the three of us left the Lake McDonald Hotel area that morning before daylight with our pack strings, a soft, wet snow was falling. I recall that some of the flakes seemed as large as half dollars. As we climbed toward Sperry Chalet, however, the air was rapidly getting colder and the snowflakes smaller. By the time we reached the chalet area, the temperature had probably fallen to zero. We estimated this from the way our breath fogged, and the air stung our faces and hands. As we topped Lincoln Pass, we were faced by a forty-mile-per-hour gale. I remember that as my head got on a level with the pass, I felt the wind hit my hat and then, as my horse climbed, my chest, then the lower part of me.

Up here it was no doubt several degrees below zero, and with that terrific wind, the chill factor was really something. From Lincoln Pass on to the campsite, a distance of four and a half miles, there was no letup whatever—in fact, as we went over the Continental Divide at Gunsight Pass and proceeded eastward that three-quarters mile, the cold gained intensity and the wind increased. At the creek crossing at the head of Lake Ellen Wilson (named for Woodrow Wilson's daughter, who had visited the area during his administration), I was walking, leading my horse, and in spite of the swiftness of the stream, the ice held my weight. From this I estimated that it had to be at least ten below zero.

When we reached the camp, Roy Holbrook, who technically was in charge of the expedition because of his seniority and because it was a camp he had serviced that we were packing out, admitted that he was just done in from the cold and wind. I could see that he would have to be gotten into a warmer place fast. He looked about like Sam Magee must have looked to Robert Service's imagination. Earl Minckler, a mechanic who had come along to disassemble a Rix Six compressor, was in even worse shape. Both had given up completely.

The author packing lumber for the construction of the Porcupine Ridge Lookout in 1939.

The Porcupine Ridge Lookout under construction in 1939. Mount Cleveland, the highest peak in Glacier National Park, is visible in the background.

Teubert was a 200-pounder, over six feet tall and only a few years older than I, and I could see that he was standing it as well as or better than I. He had, however, looked to Holbrook for guidance, and now that Roy was beaten, he looked to me for a decision as to what we should do.

Turning back was out of the question, as both Holbrook and Minckler would have been unable to survive a return trip in this blizzard in their present condition. I shuddered to think what Charles Randels would say if the three of us came back with empty pack strings, so accordingly, I took charge as though I were Mr. Randels himself. I started a fire in the cook tent stove and told the two of them to thaw out in there out of the wind. Teubert and I found spots on the lee sides of rock ledges and commenced cargoing the stacks of material.

Later, after Roy and Earl had thawed out somewhat, they made coffee and called Walt and me in for a cup. I had taken Earl's toolbox into the tent so that the tools would warm up somewhat and in hopes that Earl would take heart and at least get a start at tearing down that compressor, but he never touched a tool that day. Walt and I spent very little time in the warmth of the cook tent lest we get "unacclimated" to the blizzard outside. After coffee, I brought Roy's mantas into the tent and suggested that he cargo the groceries and cooking ware, which he did.

Walt Teubert lacked a lot in being the best packer I had seen, but I could think of none who could have equaled what he did that day in that blizzard. I had long since learned to do a fair job of cargoing and packing while wearing choppers' mitts with wool liners, and it was well that I had had lots of practice at it, as my hands would never have taken what Teubert's did as we wrapped up two stringloads under those conditions. Although we were not far apart, we were unable to see each other much of the time because of the blowing snow.

In Holbrook's string was an extra-large sorrel mule that had given him considerable trouble during the season, being hard to handle. Knowing that the cook tent, with the ice and frozen gravel that we would be unable to knock loose from it, would weigh about 300 pounds, I decided to make it into an inverted V-shape load for this mule. We folded it into a bundle nine or ten feet long and then bent it into the V, and the four of us lifted it on after all the other stock had been loaded.

Teubert's pack string was all horses, and in that string was the big bay horse, Troubadour, who had a penchant for pulling back at the most inopportune times. As we were plunging through the four-feet-deep drifts along the upper end of Lake Ellen Wilson, after dropping off the west side of Gunsight Pass, Troubadour pulled back. Teubert had his hands in his mackinaw side pockets, with the loop of his lead rope around his right hand. When Troubadour stopped, and Walt's saddle horse did not, the pocket of the coat was torn and all the buttons pulled from the front of the mackinaw. He tried holding his closed but this was not possible, and before we reached the cliffs opposite the lower end of the lake, he was really suffering. The icy wind was really getting to him. I cut an end from a cargo rope and wound it 'round him. This held his coat in place and the front closed. Both Roy and I were wearing our Stetsons, but I always carried an ear band and had donned it before we reached Sperry on our way up. Fortunately for him, Roy happened to have a necktie in his mackinaw pocket, and we cut the stitching in it with our pocket knives so it would open up into a flat ribbon. This made a suitable protection for his ears. Both Minckler and Teubert had caps with ear flaps.

Our numbness persisted, it seemed, long after we had unpacked and cared for our stock and were in Roy's cabin near the Lake McDonald Hotel. I recall that when I was going from the table to the stove with a half dozen eggs I had broken into a frying pan, to go with the ham Roy was preparing, the pan actually turned in my grip, spilling part of the eggs. Teubert was absolutely ill from the exposure he had suffered after losing his coat buttons.

Although we had got up at 4:30 that morning and were on the trail by about 6:00 a.m., and the distance was not excessively long, approximately twelve miles each way, it was well after dark when we arrived at McDonald. The weather conditions had hampered our speed in everything we did.

The spring after the Ptarmigan Tunnel was first punched through the Wall, the crew who went up to resume the work discovered that the tunnel from end to end was filled with hard-packed snow. There is a constant draft through it, and snow seems to first start building up near the midway point in it. The fall of 1932, it was decided to board up both ends of the tunnel to prevent this. Before moving the camp out, I packed five mule loads of lumber up to it for this purpose. Strissel, the camp cook, was at the south, or Many Glacier, portal as I was coming up the trail with my full string and took a photo of them. The five loads of lumber can be noted. Even with this lumber at either end, a considerable amount of snow would blow in—like snow blowing through the keyhole of a door. In later years, when I had charge of the tunnel's closure, we would put a baffle of old tent canvas about four feet in from the doors that we had installed. This caused a dead air space, and all snow would drop near the end.

The old Goathaunt Ranger Station near Waterton Lake in the winter of 1939. The station was replaced in the mid-1960s.

The Goathaunt Chalet, built in 1924 at the southern, United States end of Waterton Lake, was the only one of the Glacier National Park chalets not built by the Great Northern Railway. It was purchased by the Park Saddle Horse Company in 1925 and was part of the North Circle route until 1941. It was torn down in 1952.

When I made my last trip to Waterton that fall and moved the Pass Creek and Boundary Creek camps to Waterton station to be taken to Waterton, Alberta Townsite, and there put on a truck and taken to the warehouse, there was about ten inches of snow on the ground. A temporary (seasonal) ranger named McCormick was relieving Lou Hanson, who was taking annual leave. The morning that I left there to return to Many Glacier, it was snowing. Again I was up at 4:30 a.m. and on the trail by 6:00. It continued to snow moderately as I traveled the five miles up the Waterton Valley and the six-mile climb onward to the Fifty Mountain Plateau and the Highline Trail. When I got to the plateau, I was above the clouds and the snowing ceased. Two saddle horses from Belly River had been brought to Waterton after the horse use season there, because they could not be taken to Many Glacier via Ptarmigan—the tunnel being closed. I had inherited them for my trip back, making my string thirteen in number.

It would be hard for me to find words to adequately describe the beauty of the country around me at this time. There were about thirty inches of snow on the ground and not a cloud in the sky. The fifty or more mountain peaks for which the area is named stood out in bold relief against that solid white background. In the thirteen miles from the north edge of the plateau to Swiftcurrent Pass, the snow was never less than two and a half feet deep, and where there were drifts, it was often four feet deep. I had left Waterton riding one of the extra saddle horses from Belly River, but the horse I rode in this deep snow would tire quickly, so I would put him at the tail end of the string, where the trail was well broken, and bring my next mount up from the rear.

At Cattle Queen Creek, the snow was so deep where it had drifted that I wondered for a while if I would be able to get through. When I came to the south edge of the Ahern cirque, where the Highline Trail climbs to the level of the Granite Park Chalet, I was suddenly confronted by a long drift five or six feet deep. The side slope here was so steep that I did not feel that it would be at all safe to have an animal floundering, as he could easily roll several hundred feet to the jagged rocks below. The only tool that I had was my 3.5-pound sheath axe. At first I tried shoveling with the side of the bare double-bitted axe, but it would twist and glide in the snow and several times I narrowly missed gashing my leg with the sharp bit. With the flat side of the sheathed axe, I went to work shoveling a trail over which a horse might struggle. The snow I shoveled out on the lower side I felt would give an animal some protection from going over the side. At first I tried making a path fifty or so feet in length, then leading the saddle horse over it and then the rest of the string, but as the snow seemed to get deeper and the side hill more steep, I decided it would be best to shovel all the way across. This way an animal would not be standing where the side slope was so steep.

As I recall, I worked two and a half or three hours before I had a path that I dared try to lead a horse over. My saddle horse did considerable lunging as I led him across, but he made it okay. Next I led Tony across, with a mule following loose. After that I repeated the process of leading one animal and allowing a second to follow. I made sure that those left behind were tied to my axe handle, which I had securely packed into the snow. I did not want a wreck of any kind so far from anywhere.

I had no way of knowing, or even guessing at that time, but it would be twenty-five years before anyone would see bare ground at this spot.

The summer of 1932 had been a dry one, and the previous winter one of light snowfall. This accounted for Elmer Ness being able to ford Belly River in two places in reaching the station in his automobile. At the location of this drift, which became famous as the "Ahern Drift," I had noticed no great amount of snow in passing through during the fall. In September 1957, when we had occasion to check this drift for safety because of a horse party going through, the remaining snow had turned to blue ice. This was the smallest the drift had been since that fall of 1932.

Although I had left Waterton station at six o'clock that morning, it was dusk when I went over Swiftcurrent Pass, and I recall that as I went around the Devil's Elbow, my horse had balls of snow in his shoes six inches deep and would occasionally stumble. I was so weary that I hardly noticed, even though the sheer drop here is about seven hundred feet.

The winter of 1932–33 had been a severe one, with heavy snows and prolonged cold. Mr. Randels had put me in charge of the stock used by his division, the engineering part of the Park's operation. This amounted to nearly three-fourths of the Glacier horses and mules. They had been selected by him and Hinkley, paid for with funds appropriated to his division.

In April, he and I went to East Glacier Park by train. US Highway 2 was not kept open winter at this time, but had it been, it would have been closed by the hundreds of snow slides along the route. In the Essex, Java (Nimrod) and Fielding area, bridges had been swept from their locations and deposited against the mountainside of the opposite side of the valley. It amazed me that the Great Northern Railway had been able to keep its tracks open through all of this. All the way through the mountains from Belton (West Glacier) to East Glacier Park there were snow sheds, miles of them, protecting the tracks from these avalanches. Also, in many places were long tunnels.

One of the buildings of the Cut Bank Chalets in 1937. All traces of these buildings were removed during World War II.

The next morning, we drove on snowplowed roads to the Hudson Bay Divide eight miles south of St. Mary. On the St. Mary side of that mountain range was a crew of local residents and Park Service road crewmen hand shoveling the snow from the road way. We hiked over the pass and were met by Art Best, the St. Mary ranger. We all drove to the headquarters of the Bar-X-Six ranch, which was then located at the site of old Bureau of Reclamation Camp Nine beside the St. Mary River a mile from Babb. From there we were accompanied out on the range, where some of our stock was located, by Ross Jordan, the Bar-X-Six foreman, and Bill Heald, the summer corral boss at Many Glacier, a ranch hand the remainder of the year.

These men knew how to take us to where part of our stock was located. All were so thin and long-haired as to be almost unrecognizable. The mules had fared less well than the horses—four of them had died. Mules do not withstand the winters on open ranges like this as well as horses. Many years later at Grand Canyon, where I had charge of the Park Service horses and mules, I learned that it is the horses that suffer most when the extreme is hot weather. Mules are used there because the one-hundred-plus temperatures on the Grand Canyon trails are unbearable for horses.

Mr. Randels and I talked it over, and the decision was for me to round up our stock, take them to St. Mary, ten miles to the south, and start feeding them hay and grain. It took many trips because as soon as I had managed to round up ten or fifteen of them, I would get them to St. Mary, where they could start gaining back their strength.

W.J. Yenne on the trail south of Elizabeth Lake on Glacier's east side. This trail is part of a spectacular ride of about twenty miles that runs from Many Glacier, by way of the Ptarmigan Tunnel, into the remote and picturesque Belly River Valley and north to the Chief Mountain Customs at the Canadian border. The Belly River is one of the longest rivers in the contiguous forty-eight states to have its ultimate drainage into the Arctic Ocean by way of Hudson Bay.

Art Best gave me a lot of help, and one day we saw some Bar-X-Six cowboys moving sixty mares with foals from one location to another. It was a sight I shall never forget. As the mares trotted along, the foals were at their sides, often leaning against their mothers. It was during this roundup that I had occasion to first see the two thoroughbred remount stallions mentioned heretofore.

In May we trucked about half of the stock to Park Headquarters, where pasture grass had started well. Temporary bridges had been built across streams like Bear Creek in the Java-Fielding area, and often we would be

144

obliged to unload some of the stock and lead them across the temporary bridges because of the weight in excess of the bridges' limit.

Don Barnum, one of the fire guards, had been assigned by Paige and the chief ranger to assign stock to the various seasonal rangers and the fire guards. Don and I did a little bit of horse trading, as I needed the younger and faster saddle horses for my packers whereas he had many who needed the more quiet, dependable animals. We had a few good laughs as we discussed our trades.

Many fire trails needed to be built in the Nyack, Paola, Walton and Fielding districts that spring before the principal tourist trails were to be opened. Eight small crews were assembled, each in charge by a man who would later have a crew doing maintenance on the first class trails. I serviced all of these crews during late May, June and early July.

Because of the Depression, the U.S. government had imposed a 10 percent "economy deduction" on all appropriations as well as our salaries, so packers were not hired until badly needed. As a result, I made trips over many of the high mountain passes such as Swiftcurrent, Fifty Mountain, Triple Divide and Stoney Indian before any of the trail maintenance crews had been there.

In 1933, the 10 percent economy deduction held from our pay was increased to 15 percent. There was never a complaint from any of the employees I associated with in my work. All we need do was to look about us to see many more less fortunate people. The Great Depression was at its worst. I was happy when packers could be hired and one or two more men added to the small trail maintenance crews. The high country was still snow covered, and the high passes I had been crossing had extremely steep snowfields. These steep places would have treaded trails made across them before the saddle horse parties would use them.

Once, when I was to come south from Waterton Lake over Fifty Mountain, Jack Winkley, one of Mr. Noffsinger's guides, was going over the same route an hour behind me with a small horse party. This was July 10, and from a mile north of the Fifty Mountain plateau and across the plateau, down Mineral Creek almost to the Cattle Queen snowshoe cabin, there was solid snowcover. The winter snow was hard packed so that my stock did not sink in except where small alpine trees or large rocks were near the snow surface. At these places, the snow underneath had melted away from the tree or rock, leaving a thin snow bridge. Any animal that chanced to step there would sink nearly out of sight. Much time was lost getting them back on their feet.

Winkley was coming along an hour behind, and as he came to places where I had had one of my wrecks, he would detour.

The author's pack string and saddle horse on the snow one half mile south of the Fifty Mountain trail camp on July 10, 1933.

Near Fifty Mountain campsite, I stopped and took a photo of my empty pack string. It so happened that at almost that exact spot one of Winkley's "dudes" took a photo of him and their horses. He is a retired rancher at Rollins, on the west shore of Flathead Lake now. We have many times discussed that day and have traded photos. Winkley and I both agree that day we traveled a full nine miles over snow.

On one of my early trips on this same route, going in the opposite direction I met one of the small crews at work about three miles from Goathaunt. They were still camped at Goathaunt and told me that they would be coming to camp a bit late as they wanted to finish what they were doing. A short distance farther on, I met a very angry grizzly. He was really on the prod, so I made a detour around him. When I got to Goathaunt, I told Lou Hanson, the ranger, about it. He said that if they were unreasonably late we would take guns and go back to meet them. They got into camp at the time they had mentioned but said they had been obliged to make a wide detour around that mad grizzly.

Among the one thousand horses that were used by Mr. Noffsinger's Bar-X-Six cowboy guides were a few that were just too unreliable ("rank" was a description often used) for even a guide to take out on the mountain trails.

Some of the names I remember were Dunny, Nellie Gray, Sergeant, Yellow Hammer, Dillinger and Huguenot, along with others. These horses were "wrangle" horses, used in the early morning to round up the other horses. They were tough, tireless horses, ideal for this demanding task. The regular horse wranglers were all either men who habitually rode the "rough strings" for ranches they worked at or were professional rodeo contestants. However, the regular guides had to take their turn at times to assist in this early morning chore. Many of them told me that when they knew they were going to ride one of those spoiled horses the next morning, they had trouble sleeping.

One afternoon I was coming to Many Glacier from Belly River with a party of Park Service officials. Below Ptarmigan Lake I met a man on the trail that I had not seen before. He was riding a large brown horse with a white blotch in its forehead. We met coming around a curve, and when that big brown horse saw us he left the trail and jumped a full horse length downward into the brush below the trail. I helped the man straighten out the string of horses he was leading and learned that his name was Boone Austin and that he would be in charge of the Bar-X-Six horses at Goathaunt. Even down there in the brush that horse had done a lot of bucking.

At Goathaunt, Boone would send his horses up into the Kootenai Lake country three miles to the south to graze and would wrangle them in the morning on that brown horse. Lou Hanson and others at the ranger station told of the wild rides he would have. That horse would start bucking without warning and at any time, sometimes after Boone had ridden him a mile or two. One time when the Sierra Club was camped on the beach in front of the ranger station, the horse stampeded among their tents with Boone, bucking every inch of the way. The fellows who saw it told me that they could hear tent ropes popping and tent pegs flying. Several tents were torn down.

Boone liked me and would often ask the fellows, "When's Bill coming up again?" When I was there, he was always at my side, chatting and asking questions. Often I would repair some of his tack for him. One day, I had left Goathaunt and met Boone at a small meadow about a mile south of the ranger station. I had just my saddle horse and the one pack mule I always took along for routine freight, like having a pickup truck. Boone was bringing his horses into camp. He rode right up beside me and said, "Count 'em." I did so and said, "Twenty-eight." He kept looking at me and said, "Count 'em again."

There were some very bad bogs near Kootenai Lakes, and some of Boone's horses were mud-covered from hoof to backbone. He had come to a bog and seen them deep in the mud at a distance. He had to detour to reach where they

The author leading a horse party on the Highline Trail between Granite Park and the Ahern Drift.

had been, and by that time they were gone. Poor Boone thought they had mired out of sight. One morning, when Boone mounted the brown horse, he bucked against a forked tree near our trail crew cabins and broke his neck. He died standing up with Boone on his back. One of our packers, Bud Fox, was there. His saddle horse, a big bay, was broken to the harness, and there was a harness in the barn. They dragged the horse out into the woods and grizzly bears ate him.

In my assignment of looking after trail maintenance for the assistant engineer who had charge of them (he was busy with the construction crews), as well as the packing, I traveled much. My home was sometimes at Park Headquarters or Many Glacier, or sometimes at Two Medicine, Lake McDonald or Sun Camp. The Bar-X-Six managers were very helpful in caring for stock that I may have left for a few days when I was away. Sometimes on Sunday, when they were short of guides for one-day rides, I would guide for them in payment.

This happened at Sun Camp one day. There was a party to go up into Baring Basin and on to Sexton Glacier below Siyeh Pass. Harry Doverspike, the manager, told me that the only horse he had left for me to ride was a big bright buckskin named Yellow Hammer. Not only would Yellow Hammer buck, but he had an even worse habit of rearing up and falling over backward or over onto his side. I told Harry he would be okay. The party I had was made up of two matronly ladies, two girls of ten or twelve and three very attractive young ladies.

One of the little girls was riding a round-backed, round-bellied horse, and as we were crossing a large, very steep snowfield, I saw that her saddle was listing far over to one side. I had put the older ladies in the rear of the party, the two little girls in the middle and the young ladies up front near me for more pleasant conversation. When I glanced back from my conversation with the young lady nearest me, I saw that the girl's saddle was about to turn under the horse's belly. I quickly pulled up Yellow Hammer's reins, stepping off him as I did so.

As I left him and hurried back along the steep, hard snowfield, I could see from the corner of my eye that he had reared and was standing straight up on his hind legs. As I got beside the girl's horse, she fell on my shoulder when the saddle turned all the way. At this time, the older ladies began to chatter and ask what had happened. I just told them that I had wanted to check the saddle. Meanwhile, Yellow Hammer—not a brain in his head—had come down on all fours and had run across the snowfield to bare ground. When I got to him, the young lady who had been riding next behind me had dismounted, caught him and was holding him for me.

Contrary to the conventional wisdom of the time, all dudes are not helpless!

The Sun Camp complex at Sun Point on St. Mary Lake included the Bar-X-Six trail camp as well as the Going-to-the-Sun Chalets. The chalets were first opened by the Great Northern Railway in 1912 and were greatly expanded through the 1920s. Having fallen into disuse during World War II, they would be demolished in 1948.

## Chapter 10

# SUN CAMP AND THE TWO BEARS

There is a cabin at Sun Camp that I had occasion to occupy a lot of times. Located between Sun Point and Baring Creek on the Going-to-the-Sun Road, Sun Camp was the Bar-X-Six camp that was part of the same complex that included the Great Northern Railways' Going-to-the-Sun Chalets at Sun Point in St. Mary Lake. Once when I was there a vehicle was sent all the way from Headquarters for me. I was needed up the North Fork on the Jefferson Pass Fire. This didn't set well with me at that time because I had made commitments with two of the trail crews to be with them that week for some important phase of their work and to do some blasting for them.

As we drove over Logan Pass, I could see smoke from a fire near the east end of the Glacier Wall that extends from Heaven's Peak. I asked the ranger who had come after me what action was being taken on that fire. He was very vague, and I could sense that very little attention was being given. On questioning him I learned that a crew of CCC boys with a fire guard and a CCC foreman had gone up there a couple of times but that there was fire deep down in cracks in the cliff. Duff down there was burning, and they were unable to get to it. I pointed out a natural route for building a temporary trail up to it and explained how pumps with water vats could be placed every 1,500 feet and water could be relayed up to it.

I was on the Jefferson Fire only a few days when a call came for me to get to Headquarters on the double. Winds had come up, and that little fire on the ridge had blown up and become the famous Heaven's Peak Fire of 1936.

A fire camp was to be put in at Ahern Pass, three and a half miles north of Granite Park. I got a string of pack stock from the pasture, and through the night Tiny Powell, brother of Ace Powell, and I hauled them by truck to Logan Pass. We loaded them just at daylight with groceries, pumps, hose, mess outfits, etc., and went north along the Garden Wall section of the Highline Trail. It was touch and go the first half mile from Logan Pass along what is called the "Rimrock." Those big pump boxes were wide packs, and in order for the pack animal to clear the rock on their right there were times when their feet had to be at the very outside edge of the solid rock trail.

When we reached Ahern Pass, we had been preceded by a crew of two hundred men, overhead and two rangers; each man had carried a tool in with him. I told Tiny not to unpack until I had a chance to talk with whoever was in charge. It was quickly agreed by all that this was not the place to attack the fire. We went back to Granite Park, where the camp was set up.

Much can be, and has been, written about the Heaven's Peak Fire. It jumped the Continental Divide a short distance south of Swiftcurrent Pass and burned the ranger station, the new museum building and much of the motel at Many Glacier. It is said that had it not been for the slate roof on the big Many Glacier Hotel, it would have gone too. The densely forested area of the Swiftcurrent Valley and the lower slopes of Mount Wilbur to Iceberg Lake and Ptarmigan Falls were completely denuded.

The Bar-X-Six, with its outlying camps, located near mountain lakes, had many good fishing guides. Diamond Dick, Jack Winkley and Hank McVeigh were among the best. Red Billingsley was a very expert horseman, a top-notch rodeo rider and, with his engaging personality, was an excellent guide. He was, however, not a fishing guide. He had grown up and lived in an area where lakes and streams were few. Albert and Martha Fragner were perhaps the best fisher people among the regular summer "dudes" to come regularly to Glacier. They had been telling a young couple they knew about the wonders of Glacier's lakes and streams for fishermen.

So this couple, the Hastys, came to Glacier to fish and camp. They were expert fly fishermen, and it had been arranged for one of the better fishing guides to be at Sun Camp when they arrived and take them to Red Eagle Lake Camp. None of the better fishing guides was available when they arrived, so it was decided that Red Billingsley would guide them to the lake and a fishing guide would come in as soon as one was available.

By the time the party reached the camp, the Hastys had become well acquainted with Red and had learned to like him. When they went out to fish, they insisted that Red go along. He told me afterward how he made

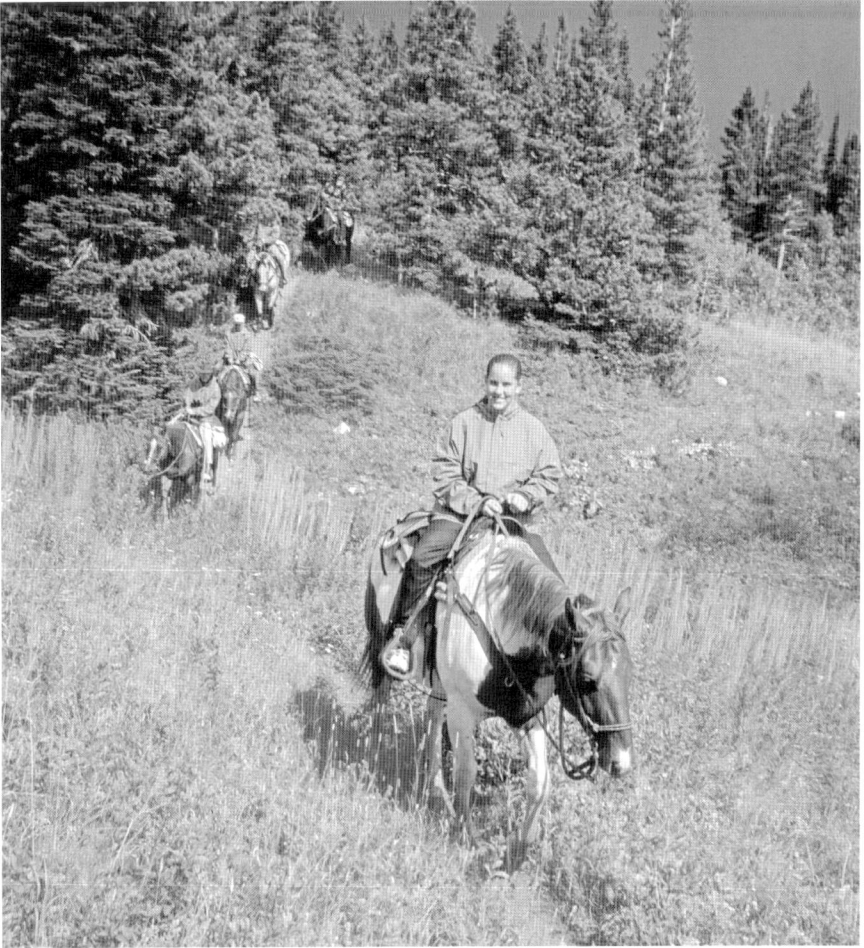

The author's granddaughter Annalisa on the Poia Lake Trail near Many Glacier in 1996. *W.P. Yenne.*

every excuse he could think of to avoid going and exposing his ignorance of fly fishing to these experts. Of course he used the excuse that he had no fishing rod. George Aahl, the camp manager, shot that down by offering to lend his rod. When Red ran out of excuses, he reluctantly took Aahl's rod and went with them.

Red was a quick thinker with a keen sense of humor, so he used his best weapon. When they started to tie a fly to his line, he noticed that a white butterfly had landed on a bush nearby. He said to the Hastys, "You don't think you can fool those trout with something like that do you?" Thereupon he caught the butterfly and attached it to the hook. On his first awkward cast, one of the largest cutthroat trout to be caught that summer took his bait. Red told me afterward that he was absolutely thunderstruck when he saw the size of that trout. He did not know what to do next. He did not use his reel, he just turned and started walking hastily away from the water, leading the fish.

The Hastys, seeing the size of the fish, stopped their fishing and started shouting instructions to Red. When he reached the brush back from the edge of the lake, he laid his pole down and turned and started back to the water's edge, going hand over hand down his line, taking up the slack and pulling the fish in. When Red picked the fish up out of the water, Mr. and Mrs. Hasty were at his side and helped take it off the hook. They were visibly impressed by its size. With his quick wit, Red had to add a little extra, so when the fish was off the hook he said, "Shucks, you don't keep little ones like this do you?"

He then made as though he were going to throw it back into the lake. With this, both of the Hastys tackled him like a football player. All three lay there on the lakeshore laughing so hard they were unable to get up.

When they had left Sun Camp for Red Eagle Lake, I had been there, as the Bar-X-Six horse camp was adjacent to my cabin and corral, and Red had introduced me to them. He had told them nice things about me, many of which I wished were true. The afternoon that they arrived back at Sun Camp, they looked me up and suggested that the four of us, including Red, go to Many Glacier to the dance that night. All the way to Many Glacier they laughed about the cutthroat trout incident. Their itinerary included other camps and other lakes, and now good fishing guides had become available, but they would have none other than Red.

MY CABIN IN THE Sun Camp (now Sun Point) area was of logs, clean and new, just a single room. On either side was a very large window. Because this was the domain of the bear, both black and grizzly, heavy iron bars had been put on the windows. The windows were side hinged, and I often left them a bit ajar for ventilation. One time when I was away for a few days, a small black yearling bear managed to climb through between the bars and got into some of my food. Guides riding by to their camp next door saw him through the window, unlocked the cabin and chased him out.

The next summer, that same bear, along with his twin brother, was back. Several times those two managed to get through the bars and into my cabin.

The guides knew where I cached the key, as they often would lock some of their things there. A couple of times they saw one of the bears in there as they rode by and would unlock the door and chase him out. Each time the bear made shambles of my groceries. Of course word had spread to the chalets, which employed thirty or more young people. When I'd go down there in the evenings, I would be plagued with inquiries as to whether I was afraid. In leaving the chalets after an evening there, I'd say, "Guess I'll go home and put the bears out and go to bed." Or I would complain what a hard time I was having, supporting myself and two bears on my small salary.

Green suits were in vogue, and I had one. Once, when the guides reported that the bears had messed my cabin up, and I was not due back for a couple of days, two of the girls went up there and cleaned it up for me. They found my green suit on the floor. Later, at the chalets, when they told me about finding my new suit on the floor, I replied, "Yeah, you know, the other night I woke up and one of them bears was trying the vest on."

Sun Camp was eighteen miles from Many Glacier by trail, and the young people who worked at these places would often hitchhike to the other of the places and then hike back over Piegan Pass. One day, two nineteen-year-old lads working at Many Glacier did this. They had been given a ride to Piegan Underpass (also Jackson Glacier Overlook) and were hiking from there.

Upon reaching Preston Park, they saw three bears, two of them cubs, cross the trail ahead of them. When they reached that point, a female grizzly dashed out of the brush and knocked down one of the lads, John Daubney. The angry bear slashed at John's chest and sides, his thighs, bit him on the side of his neck and on one ear. He was protecting his face with his forearms, and they too received serious wounds. He told me later that the most horrible pain was when she bit his thighs. After a while, she stepped back a few paces and just looked at him. He then staggered to his feet, and he told me that he kicked her on the jaw. She then went into the brush where her cubs were. John called to his friend, who had run up the trail onto the shale side of Cataract Mountain. He came back and helped John back down to the trail to the Going-to-the-Sun Road. There they managed to catch a ride back to Sun Camp Chalet.

There, besides Miss Roach, the resident nurse, was a surgeon who happened to be a guest. He took 101 stitches in patching John up. John was a courageous boy, and when he was out of the anesthetic, he began asking questions as to what he should have done in a situation such as this. They told him that there was a Park Service man who lived in a cabin near there who knew more about bears than anyone else. They said this man actually

A grizzly (*Ursus arctos horribilis*) in the high country of Glacier National Park. *National Park Service photo.*

lived with bears a part of the time in his cabin and had no fear of them. (This speaks well for the many yarns I had been telling them about myself and those twin black bears.) John said he wanted to talk with that man.

That evening, when I went to the chalets, I was immediately led to his room. I answered his every question truthfully to the best of my knowledge. Even told him that my knowledge was far less than he had been led to believe. He acted as though he would rather believe the others. I spent many evenings with him in his room. His parents had been notified, and his mother came from St. Paul by train at once.

John told her about me with my vast knowledge about all things pertaining to wild animals, and of course she wanted to meet me and get my version. This was in 1939.

In 1968, twenty-nine years later, and the year after the two grizzly killings in Glacier that inspired Jack Olsen's book, *Night of the Grizzlies*, my wife was going to Minneapolis to visit her two brothers. I had heard that John

Daubney had become a prominent attorney and had been the mayor of St. Paul. I asked my wife to see what she could find out about him. When she told the story to her sister-in-law, the latter got interested and in no time had John on the phone for her. When my wife identified herself, John said, "Yes, I remember Bill Yenne very well," and went on to tell her all about our conversations in his room. He said that his son, Tom Daubney, had been working at Lake McDonald Lodge (previously Lake McDonald Hotel) in Glacier the previous year with Michele Koons, the second of the two girls to be killed on August 13, 1967, during the infamous "night of the grizzlies."

Tom Daubney had written his parents for permission to hike and camp in the backcountry on his days off. The hotel company required this permission for minors because of the dangers. John told my wife that the same day they received his letter, the newspapers, radio and television were full of the news of the two girls having been killed. The Daubneys then not only refused him permission but also had advised that he come home. In almost a lifetime of working in grizzly country, I have had more than my share of close calls with them.

I well know how a grizzly scare can stay with you for a long time.

The author (*foreground*) and his wife, Doris Kathleen Cunningham Yenne, at the head of the Bright Angel Trail during a ride that took them to the bottom of the Grand Canyon in November 1948. Behind them are the author's sister, Frances, and her husband, John Clinton "Barney" Gudgel.

## Chapter 11

# POSTWAR YEARS AT GRAND CANYON

D uring World War II, I was away from the National Park Service. The navy kept me out of the army, and a subpar left hand, the result of a hay mowing machine accident in early childhood, kept me from any real action and from crossing any of the oceans.

Later, I worked at Todd-Pacific Shipyards in Seattle as a welder and eventually a welding instructor and foreman, working on Fletcher Class destroyers. I was aboard one such destroyer at Harbor Island on February 18, 1943, and, looking across the water, watched as the top-secret second prototype Boeing XB-29 bomber, with Boeing's top test pilot, Edmund T. "Eddie" Allen, crashed into the Frye Packing Plant. Allen and all other members of this highly technical crew aboard died in the crash and the fire that followed.

Not long after returning to the Park Service in Glacier, I was transferred to Grand Canyon National Park. There, my duties were to have charge of the maintenance of all buildings, water systems and of flood control features—flood control because of the summer cloudbursts. I was in charge of rim walk and trail maintenance and of course had charge of the Park Service horses and mules. Later, because of an accident to the electrician foreman, I assumed maintenance of the cross-canyon telephone lines. I had a small crew stationed on the South Rim at Park Headquarters, where I lived. There were also crews at Indian Gardens, Cottonwood, the North Rim (in summer only) and at Rock House. The latter was at the river near Phantom Ranch, which was operated by the Fred Harvey Company, which also ran the mule concession that took parties down into the canyon on the world-famous Bright Angel and Kaibab Trails.

The winter of 1948–1949 was the most severe winter since records had been kept in that part of the Southwest. Both my Park Service pack string and those of the Fred Harvey Company were stationed at Yaki Point, three and a half miles east of Grand Canyon Village and Park Headquarters. There were no tourist mule parties, so that the Bright Angel Trail was having practically no use. I had moved my crews from both Cottonwood and Indian Gardens to the South Rim. In the canyon, I had only the small crew at Rock House. The Park Service packer lived at Yaki Point, as did the Fred Harvey packers.

As more snow fell, and the switchbacks at the heads of the trails had to be hand shoveled for the pack mules to get through, I needed all the men I could muster. At places the snow on either side of the narrow passage we had shoveled was as high as the backs of the mules. It seemed that there was a blizzard every afternoon, when the trails had to be opened to permit the pack strings to get out of the canyon. Of course, we had to be out there in the early morning for the same purpose.

John Bradley, the Fred Harvey mule boss, came to me with a proposition. He said that if I would move my pack string to the village and use only the Bright Angel Trail, he would do the same. He also said that when shoveling was necessary, he would send his crew to help my men. He added, "And I'll be there with them." He was as good as his word, and no man shoveled any more snow in a day than he did.

Meanwhile, Bob Cavnes, my trail foreman down at Rock House, became very ill with pneumonia, a lung congestion and kidney infection. The doctor in the village refused to go down into the canyon, telling me that he would have to be brought out. Word spreads quickly in a place like that, especially in winter when there are no tourists. Everyone knew of my problem. The chief ranger and the assistant superintendent came to my house and told me that they would get me as many men as I would need to help carry him out.

I knew that in that narrow passage the last two miles coming out, it would be impossible for men to carry a stretcher. I told them that in the plan I had there would be need for only one man to help me, and that Ben Meadows, the best-qualified man that I could think of, had already volunteered. Ben was a Park Service equipment operator in the road crew. He was also an expert horseman and, importantly for this mission, a very strong man.

Late that evening, when I was in the barn fastening a Stokes litter to a packsaddle, Ben came and asked me what time in the morning I wanted him

Riders descending into the Grand Canyon on the South Kaibab Trail. The author supervised crews on all of the canyon's trails.

to report at the barn. I told him five o'clock. The next morning, at 4:30 a.m., I went to the barn and found he had already caught and grained the stock I had told him we would use for the rescue trip.

On the way down, we had left some soup in a thermos and other items at Indian Gardens. The doctor had given me some drugs to give him, morphine I think. Arriving at Indian Gardens, we got the foreman into the house after it had a chance to warm up. I had built a quick fire. There was no way he wanted to arrive at the South Rim riding in that Stokes litter, so he was transferred to his regular mule that we had brought along from Rock House. When we got to the rim, there were about two hundred people there watching us arrive.

Maintenance of trails and water systems had fallen far behind, so there was much to be done in a hurry. One thing we needed badly was more pack stock. I felt also a need to upgrade packing methods. The purchasing officer and I wrote and phoned far and wide to find where we could find suitable mules to purchase. No luck. I had heard that in the ranch country in Utah some ranchers raised a few. My wife and I went over to the North Rim, and I made trips up into Utah each day. At Cedar City and at Hurricane I found just the type of mules I was looking for, purchasing two at each location. The problem was that all were seven-years-old, the youngest I could find in my travels, and none had had a rope on him since he was branded and gelded. They were totally unbroken. It is harder to break an animal when they are that old, but in a day and a half at the North Rim, I had them all pretty well halter broken.

My Dad had taught me well. On the third day, I started out on the twenty-one-mile trip across the canyon on the Kaibab Trail with them. In the "Devil's Back Yard" below the North Rim are 1,800-foot drop-offs, but I made the fourteen miles to Rock House without incident.

I stayed all night at Rock House and the next morning got them saddled without difficulty. I had always to work from the front because they would kick any time they thought they might be able to hit me. Bob Cavnes, now the trail boss there, helped me take them across the suspension bridge across the Colorado River at the bottom of the canyon and through the 120-foot-long tunnel at the end of the bridge. In riding through this tunnel, one can touch the rock on either side or overhead without fully extending the arm.

When I had arrived at the North Rim a few days before with these unbroken seven-year-old mules, there had been much talk and some doubt as to my chances of ever getting them halter broken and across the canyon.

During the day and a half I had spent halter breaking them, I had many kibitzers and doubting spectators.

Word had spread to Phantom Ranch and to the South Rim that I was going to attempt crossing the canyon alone with four "bronc" mules. When I had stayed the night at Rock House, I had spent the evening at Phantom Ranch. Three mule parties with their guides were also there. The manager at the ranch had told me that all three guides had expressed doubts as to my success in getting those mules to Yaki Point.

In crossing the Kaibab Bridge and going through the tunnel, none of the mules had attempted to pull back. I had given those that I thought might do so to Cavnes to lead. I had come behind leading the other two, with some walnut-sized rocks in hand to throw at those ahead should they refuse to go. All went well.

The first three were wearing packsaddles and were tied together, as is the rule for pack stock. This prevents any from doubling back or coming forward and crowding another off the trail. As I had done the day before, I gauged my speed in rounding switchbacks so that all kept moving. Had I gone a trifle too quickly, one would be caught before he had rounded it and would then be obliged, by the pull on his lead rope, to double back on the same (lower) side of the switchback. Had I gone too slowly, it would give one a chance to come to a complete stop.

In all of this I had had lots of practice. At Cedar Ridge on the Kaibab Trail, I passed the three parties that I had seen at Phantom Ranch. I was jubilant at the success I had had so far, so when they all stared at me as I went past, and were talking and pointing, it bothered me not. Above Cedar Ridge was a sheer cliff area and some more switchbacks. Ahead of one of the switchbacks, the trail made a half circle curve in a cliff area, making my rear vision impossible.

There, for the first and only time, the last mule failed to round the switchback. I could not see him and had no inkling that I was having a wreck until I heard the noise of a struggle and could see the third mule's head straining forward. The mules had all become very excited and were straining forward on the taut halter ropes of the mule behind them. In just a moment the second and third mules fell over because of the side pull caused by the small radius of the curve in the trail. I had put the largest, and kickingest, of them in front, directly behind me. He was still standing.

I knew that I could never get back past him alive because on the left was a forty-foot sheer drop while on the right was the sheer wall. I reined my saddle animal in tight to the cliff, took a dally on the saddle horn and

Switchbacks through the redwall limestone on Grand Canyon's Bright Angel Trail above Indian Gardens.

jerked that one off his feet. Now all three of them were lying with their backs to the wall, unable to get up because their heads were stretched forward by the halter ropes.

All were breathing hard. I was able to walk to the rear over the sides of the fallen animals and cut the rope of the caboose mule. He had been led about fifteen feet back down the trail and was standing with his head elevated so high that his front feet were barely touching the ground. As I led him around the switchback, I saw a good-sized branch lying in the trail. It had been given to one of the dudes by their guide to make their mule keep up and had been lost. Through all of this my main thought was of all the people who had been saying I'd never make it across.

A plan came to my mind. I was thinking of those three guides behind me and the laughs if they had a chance to tell of my wreck. It was not too difficult to tie the caboose mule to the saddle of the third mule. I stepped over him to his head and cut his rope so he could get up. Then, standing at his shoulder, I uncinched and righted his saddle and tied him to the second mule lying there helpless. I then walked over that mule and went through the same sequence until all were on their feet, saddled and ready to go. As I worked my way back to my saddle animal, I used that branch to brush out all of my footprints and other evidence of a struggle.

Arriving at Yaki Point, I decided to take them on to Park Headquarters at Grand Canyon Village. Much of that three-and-a-half-mile trail parallels the road closely, and Ben Meadows, the man who the winter before had helped me with my rescue, and his foreman, driving by, saw me. When I arrived at the barn and corrals, they were waiting. They had been hearing the news of my trip and had heard of the doubts. They praised my choice in selecting these animals and congratulated me on successfully doing the impossible. I then told them about my wreck, just as I've told it here, but swore them to secrecy. To my knowledge, they never told anyone.

[Editor's note: In a November 1988 letter to his friend Jack Dollan, W.J. Yenne recalled, "When I wrote *Switchback* the spring of 1983, I had forgotten how high the drop-off was where I had been taking those bronc mules across the Canyon. I didn't want to exaggerate as I knew Grand Canyon people would be reading it, so I said 40 feet. In the fall of 1983, when I passed by, I could see that it was nearer 200 feet. Coming out again this year, the two guides and I looked it over and agreed it was about 200 feet."]

The only packer I had at Grand Canyon in the late 1940s was not a good hand with stock, so I would not let him work with the Utah mules. I kept them and hired a cowboy-packer named John O'Day to work with me in gentling them and breaking them to the saddle. After they were broken, he continued to work with the packer, as two strings were needed.

During a three-month period shortly after this, I was without a packer. Supplying of our inner canyon stations had fallen far behind so that when I made a trip down with supplies, I packed seven or eight mules instead of the standard of five used there. I also hauled bigger loads. In here are photos of my pack string. It included the young mules I had just bought.

One Sunday evening, my foreman at Indian Gardens phoned me to chat about his work in that section. He told me that a man had come there that forenoon asking how far it was to the river and how far to the Kaibab Bridge. It was beastly hot in the canyon at that time, but he said the man was wearing a tweed suit and had the coat on. After getting directions, he had hurried on down the trail.

The next day, John O'Day and I went to Cottonwood Camp, seven miles above Phantom Ranch toward the North Rim. At Phantom Ranch as we were coming back the next day, we were told that a man in Albuquerque, New Mexico, had left a suicide note on his office desk saying he was going to the bottom of Grand Canyon and jump off the Kaibab Bridge. The sheriff there had called park officials at Grand Canyon, and all points had been alerted to be on the lookout for him. He matched the description of the man that Davis, my foreman, had told me about.

After we had crossed the river that day and were on the River Trail going to the lower end of the Bright Angel Trail, I saw a piece of notebook paper, weighted down by a rock, lying on the wall at the outside edge of the trail. I was riding one of the new mules so I decided it best not to reach for it or get off my mule. John was riding ahead of me, leading the pack animals. I called to him and told him of the paper. He had seen it also. A short time later, he called to me and pointed to another piece of paper weighted down in the same manner beside the trail. That time, I got off my mule and retrieved it. It was from a five-by-eight spiral notebook but entirely blank.

At Indian Gardens, I had planned flood control work and was increasing the size of the crew. Mrs. Davis was hired to cook for the crew. In discussing plans with her that day, she said she would need four more chairs for seating the men at the dining table. We decided on folding chairs because they could be put out of the way when not in use. I wrote on the notebook paper I had found, "Folding chairs, Indian Gardens." I gave the paper to Howard Stricklin, the chief ranger who had been in constant contact with the sheriff in Albuquerque. In a letter to Howard a few days later, he said that the paper was from the same pad as the suicide note but added, "The four words written on it 'folding chairs Indian Gardens' are not in his handwriting."

WHEN WE WERE MOVING to Grand Canyon, my wife and I drove to the North Rim for a look at the canyon. Large herds of mule deer were everywhere. I told my wife that night at Marble Canyon, where we stayed, that we must have seen 350 deer in that forty-mile drive. The next day at Park Headquarters, in talking with two rangers who had been on that road the same time we were, they told me that they had counted 450.

At Cottonwood Camp, a very large mule deer buck came often in the evenings. I was told that he had been there as a fawn with his parents. One time I went there and saw that he was limping badly. He had stepped into a two-inch galvanized pipe coupling, left over from the phone line construction. The telephone poles and the cross arms were of two-inch pipe.

The author in the lead, returning from his rescue of a gravely ill man from the bottom of the Grand Canyon on February 23, 1949. *National Park Service, photo by Jim Eden.*

Eddie Howell, my trail boss stationed there, and I concocted a plan for getting that fitting off the buck's foot. I tied two cargo ropes together, then we fastened one end to the outer end of a stout branch of a large willow tree near the buildings. When the deer came, I roped him around his large antlers—it would have been hard to miss a rack like that. When the rope struck him, he was off like a shot. When he hit the end of the rope tied to that springy branch, the force threw him down, and he landed beside a large boulder about six feet high. As soon as he landed, I shouted and told Eddie to get on his head.

This done, I tied a rope around his hind feet, took it around the rock and tied the other end to his front foot, the one without the coupling. This done, I went to work to free the coupling. Darkness was coming, so I sent Eddie's helper for a Coleman lantern. Next I sent him after a squirt can of oil. Still I was having no luck. While I worked at that coupling, I told the boys that all my life, no matter what I happened to be doing, I had always felt that somewhere someone was doing exactly the same thing at the same time as I. "Right now," I told them, "I don't think that is the case." The coupling finally came off. We washed the foot thoroughly with a Lysol solution. In a few days, he was back around the camp.

A couple of days after I had arrived at Grand Canyon, and was still being shown around, I was in the naturalist workshop where Louie Shellback and Ernst Christiansen were showing me some very fine displays they had made two or three years before to be put up at the "River House," a shelter at the lower end of the Bright Angel Trail near the Colorado River. They had two sheets of plate glass four feet by seven feet each. The originals down there had been destroyed by vandals. The plate glass for the originals had been carried down in relays by CCC boys. I asked them why the delay in getting the new displays and glass down there. They told me that both the Park Service and Fred Harvey packers had told them that it would be impossible to pack the glass down there without breaking it. When I expressed surprise at that, they asked me if it could be done, and I told them it would not be difficult. They then begged me to do it for them.

I found two sheets of old discarded half-inch plywood, cut it to the length of the glass and put a light frame around them to hold the glass in place. Then I nailed two short pieces of four-by-six planks to them, these to set vertical against the saddle to hold the whole thing out from the mule so as not to bother his head or bump his hip. As the saddles were sawbucks, all I had to do was staple a couple of short rope loops to them and the whole thing, glass and all, could be just hung on the mules. To balance each one on the opposite sides of the mules were the crates of displays. At the River House, I helped the two young seasonal naturalists to put them up and then cleaned up the mess that had been a long time in accumulating. Hikers and mule parties had been eating their lunches here, and nobody had bothered to police it up.

I burned everything combustible, putting all the cans and foil in a pile to be packed out as I went. There were gobs of black and gray ashes that I decided to take down and throw in the river. A million tons of silt passed by there every twenty-four hours, so a few ashes would not hurt anything, I figured. I put them all in mantas, put them on the two pack mules and started the one hundred yards to the river. There were seven or eight mule parties and all had finished their lunches and had hiked down for a look at the river. I met them a little way from the river's edge as they were starting back. I noticed that they stared at me with a sort of astonishment and I wondered why. After all, they had ridden a mule down there, so seeing me riding and leading two mules should not astonish anyone. They all stepped aside as I went by, and then I heard them saying to one another, "He's going to cross the river."

The river here was eight hundred feet wide and swift. When they asked if that were true, I told them that I was, but that my stock was tired and I would rest them for about forty-five minutes. Those guides had an extremely hard time getting their dudes on the mules for the trip back. They bawled me out for a month over that.

About a month later, I was leaving the South Rim about eleven o'clock in the forenoon, the pack string and crews having left three hours earlier. I was riding a very playful mule named Pima. He was the one my wife always rode on her trips into the canyon with me. I got to Jacob's Ladder a little after twelve and started to eat my lunch on the go. I wrapped the reins around the saddle horn, clamped my gloves under my armpit and got my sack lunch from the saddlebags. As I was holding the bag in one hand and a sandwich in the other, Pima suddenly broke into a gallop down the trail. He had been showing some impatience to catch up with the other stock, but this burst of speed was unexpected. He went around three or four of the switchbacks and was headed for a particularly steep one that I figured we had not a chance in the world of getting around alive at that speed.

Meanwhile, I had been getting myself in a position to slow him down without sacrificing my lunch or losing my gloves. Just when I began to wonder how this was going to turn out, Pima suddenly slowed to a walk. Down below, I could see about thirty hikers standing watching us. As I passed by

The author with a pack string transporting hay to Phantom Ranch at the bottom of the Grand Canyon on September 19, 1949. *National Park Service.*

them a little while later, one man said, "Mister, you sure do ride fast on these trails." I imagined I could hear Pima chuckle.

As I approached the head of the Bright Angel Trail one morning to go into the canyon, I paused to wait for a mule party that had been mounted and was being given riding and safety instructions by their guide. A large man in the party wearing a large western hat spoke to the guide. I recognized his voice: it was John Wayne. He told the guide that he was an experienced horseman and that if in any way he could be of assistance, he would be happy to help out. The guide replied that since he wished to help, it would be appreciated if he would "bring up the drag," that is, ride behind the party so as to see, or foresee, any trouble. He rode behind.

After they had rounded the first switchback and were passing beneath me, the guide looked up at me, waved and called me by name. When he saw that his party were all looking up also, he told them about me, what my job was there and some things about my past. I stayed a polite distance behind until Wayne stopped his mule and waited for me to catch up. We chatted for the next hour and a half until we reached Indian Gardens, where the party stopped for a rest and I continued on.

John Wayne shook my hand when we parted.

W.J. Yenne (*leading the pack string*) and a horse party at Ptarmigan Lake in 1966. The Ptarmigan Wall is in the background. The trail leading to the Ptarmigan Tunnel is visible on the hillside, but the tunnel itself is out of the frame to the right.

## Chapter 12

# BACK AT GLACIER

In 1951, I transferred from Grand Canyon back to Glacier. For nearly two decades after that, I directly supervised the maintenance of Glacier's backcountry infrastructure, maintaining for many years 1,080 miles of trails. I would have to say that if you traveled those trails during that period, you no doubt met me back there somewhere. I had the privilege of supervising hundreds of the finest young men that this country has ever produced. I am still in contact with many of them. They came from most of the states. One year thirty-nine states were represented in my crews. I was later also given responsibility for supervising all of Glacier's roads, including the famous fifty-mile Going-to-the-Sun Road, and I was park safety officer in Glacier for five years.

When I first got back from Grand Canyon, the trails were not all in good shape. The trail on the west side of Hidden Lake around the shoulder of Mount Clements had sloughed off to where there was no trail at all. People hiking had to walk on a hard gravelly side hill. In October, after the tourist season, I took a crew and a small Oliver-Cletrac crawler tractor up there to begin the work of rebuilding the trail. It was a small tractor, only about three feet wide, for use in narrow small spaces like mountain trails.

As we were unloading the tractor on Logan Pass, two carloads of Canadian ranchers pulled up. They got out of their cars and started complaining about the weather, which was dark and gloomy, though it was not snowing. They pointed out the trees, which are rarely taller than around six feet or so up on the Continental Divide, and suggested that there must have been a recent forest fire. I explained that this was timberline. The summers are short and the winters are long, so concerning the alpine fir—I mentioned their Latin name, *Abies laciocarpa*—I told them "that's all the taller our trees get." They shook their heads and seemed amused.

To distract them, I pointed out some mountain goats up on Clements, and they went off to look at them. When they returned, I had just finished unloading the little tractor. They were familiar with large crawler tractors, such as a Caterpillar D7 or D8, but they had never seen one this size. They were just overwhelmed by how small my tractor was, and they started kidding me about it. I just shook my head and told them, "You know how it is with these short summers and long winters. Our tractors just don't get any bigger."

In 1953, I got a letter from the superintendent of Yellowstone National Park offering me a ranger job, and he suggested that I come down and take a look. I thought it would be pretty nice to get out of the kind of clothes I'd been wearing and put on a uniform. They offered me the Wapiti district on the east side, where the road goes out to Cody, Wyoming. I would have four seasonal rangers and one permanent ranger working under me. I went down to look it over but decided not to take the job, because at that time, my son was three years old and I didn't like the idea of my family living way off in the boondocks. I was later offered a similar job at Hawaii Volcanoes National Park but declined for the same reason.

At about 4:30 in the afternoon on May 23, the day after we returned from Yellowstone to West Glacier, where we owned a house just outside the Park, the neighbor lady came to our door and said there had been a terrific snow slide up on the Going-to-the-Sun Road. Some of the men who were in the crew opening the road for the season had been swept downhill and were buried alive. I had the day off, but I went over to Park Headquarters, where Assistant Chief Ranger Len Coughlin put me in charge of a convoy that was taking some Great Northern Railway section crews up to help dig in the slide.

I passed the Garden Wall Road Camp, about three quarters of a mile from the slide, and led the convoy up. Just after I arrived, I ran into Dimon "Dimie" Apgar, whose family founded the little village of Apgar at the foot of Lake McDonald. He was just telling me that the men who had been digging all afternoon were cold and exhausted and about ready to give up when someone spotted a patch of brown hair.

Everyone gathered around, and somebody radioed for Dr. W.F. Bennett of Columbia Falls, who was down at the Garden Wall Road Camp. He told

The author (*right*) with Roy Bengtson and Clyde Fauley with a snowplow near Avalanche Creek during the opening of the Going-to-the-Sun Road in April 1960. In addition to being the supervisor of backcountry trails in Glacier, W.J. Yenne was in charge of Glacier's roads.

them to uncover the man as much as possible but not to move him. They followed his instructions and found longtime park employee Eugene Michael Sullivan, who had been buried for seven and a half hours. With Bennett's help, they got him down to the road camp, thawed him out and took him to the hospital in Kalispell.

I stayed all night. It was an awfully bad night. It was practically freezing, and in the sleet and gathering darkness, men were digging in the snow for those who were still buried. Of the four men caught in the avalanche, Fred Klein also survived but was badly injured. Bill Whitford and George Beaton were killed.

In 1914, the Great Northern Railway had opened chalets at Sperry and Granite Park Chalets in Glacier's backcountry. After World War II, travel habits had changed and the company decided it could no longer make money with these mountain chalets accessible only by trail, so in the winter of 1952–1953 it sold them to the National Park Service for a dollar apiece. In fact, it forced them on the Park Service.

In the spring of 1953, Glacier's superintendent, Jack Emmert, along with his assistant and the chief ranger, called me in. By now, I was maintenance supervisor of all the backcountry trails in Glacier, and they wanted to know whether I had any idea about the operation of those chalets because they figured that I knew a little more about the backcountry than any of them, and I had a trail crew at both locations.

Between us, a plan came together that the trail crews would live in the chalets. We would not open them for overnight stays but would run a concession to sell things to people who camped in the campgrounds near the chalets. I added another man to each crew and made up some signs for the door of each chalet with a list of food we had for sale, like pork and beans, small cans of fruit and cookies. We also got some little things with a grill and a pan for charcoal briquettes. The signs explained that our store would open each afternoon at around 2:30 p.m.

My trail boss at Sperry was Mike Lacy. He was the son of Marion Lacy, a well-regarded photographer in Whitefish. He was a really capable young man with a good personality who was an engineering student in college, and he operated Sperry Chalet under my direction in 1953. Ralph Fitzpatrick was my trail boss at Granite Park Chalet.

Meanwhile, there were two people who were interested in taking over permanent operations at the two chalets for the following year. One was a man who was well known in the Park for writing letters to congressmen, senators and the secretary of the interior complaining about how Glacier Park operated. The other man was Ross Luding, who operated a café in Martin City, near the Park's west entrance. He was well liked and had a good reputation, so when he and his wife, Kay, expressed interest, the Park Service from Washington to West Glacier wooed them. The Ludings began operating Sperry and Granite Park Chalets in 1954. [Editor's note: Their family operated them until 1992.]

EACH FALL, AS THE trail crews finished their work for the season, we would have four or five head of horses at places throughout the Park—such as at Polebridge, Waterton, Belly River and Walton—with larger numbers in our pack strings at Headquarters and at St. Mary. As we were through with our stock, we would take them all to St. Mary, pull the shoes off and turn them out to Red Eagle Meadows, where there are several hundred acres of nice grass. They would graze there until we were ready to take them to winter range out on the Blackfeet Reservation, where ranchers would bid on wintering our stock. I would go over each fall to inspect the winter range and round up the horses.

One year, when I went over to St. Mary, I learned that one of our horses had been injured so badly that he had to be destroyed out in the pasture. The next morning, when I went out with Don Barnum, the St. Mary ranger, to begin rounding up the stock, the carcass of the dead horse was still near the trail where he had been shot. As we rode, the ranger was telling me where he would be, and I was looking past him, trying to see the animal. It had snowed about an inch or an inch and a half the night before, and the aspens had shed about half their leaves.

As I leaned out to look around Barnum, who was ahead of me, I couldn't see anything that looked like a chestnut-colored horse, but in the distance,

The author on the trail east of Triple Divide Pass on August 11, 1962, with Triple Divide Peak, at the intersection of the Continental Divide and the Hudson Bay Divide, directly behind him.

I could see an unusual mound of dirt and an animal that was about the same size as a horse, but it was dark brown. About the time I glimpsed this and realized that it was a bear, he raised up on its hind feet and put his paw against an aspen. I estimated that he stood about nine feet tall.

People talk about grizzlies that can make a track fourteen inches long with their hind feet. I told Don Barnum that if there ever was a grizzly who could make a track like that, this was him. I told Don that I was going to try to find a track in the snow and see how big it was. However, the bear had the snow all tramped down, and it was impossible to see a clear track.

I investigated the pile of dirt, leaves and snow and found it about ten feet long, three feet high and five feet wide. That grizzly had completely covered the dead horse except for the thigh, where he had been feeding on the red meat. Hunters often find that when they kill and dress an elk and come back the next day to take it out, a grizzly will have found it during the night and covered it like this.

As I was looking for a track, Don kept saying that I ought to get out of there. The big griz was still a short distance away, running back and forth and getting angry, so I cleared out.

Through the rest of the day, I was gathering about eight to a dozen head of horses at a time and bringing them into the barn and corrals at St. Mary. Each time I came near the grizzly, he would chase the stock out into the woods.

That night, a bunch of people gathered at the ranger station for a card party. Among them were a couple of rangers from the west side of the Park to take part in the twenty-five-mile stock drive to winter range. One of them was Harold Estey, who had worked at Yellowstone for several years and who later went back there as chief ranger. As I recounted the story of the nine-foot grizzly, these rangers kidded me, saying that "every time old Bill tells a grizzly story, the grizzly gets bigger."

"All right you guys," I told them. "Tomorrow we'll go up there."

The next morning, I saddled and fed five horses before breakfast. Dick's wife, Grace Barnum, was quite an outdoors lady and had said she wanted to go with us, but she changed her mind overnight. The two rangers from the west side, and another St. Mary ranger, Hugh Buchanan, who had been in Glacier since 1928, rode up with me.

I was scared to death that the grizzly wouldn't be there, but he was in exactly the same spot as the day before, and it happened just like it had the day before. When we got close, he stood up and put his paw against a tree. I motioned to the other guys to ride up close to me and to be quiet. I just sat there on my horse and said over and over, "Is that bear nine feet tall?"

W.J. Yenne leading an official party near timber line in the Glacier National Park high country on June 9, 1969. For most of his career with the National Park Service, only rangers and ranger-naturalists wore uniforms. By this time, senior personnel on the engineering side of operations were authorized to be in uniform.

The author near Gunsight Lake in August 1979, with Going-to-the-Sun Mountain in the distant background. *Omer Raup.*

None of them could say anything but to express their awe—and their agreement that the bear was at least nine feet tall. When the grizzly dropped down and ambled off, Harold Estey, who was familiar with the huge grizzlies in Yellowstone, added that this bear was at least three feet wide.

THROUGH THE YEARS, I held supervisory positions on many large forest fires. In 1958, I was a division boss on the Coal Creek Fire in Glacier. Joseph L. "Bill" Orr, chief ranger at Big Bend National Park, came as liaison officer with the Southwest Indian firefighters. With them, we spent time at a drop camp high up on Wolf Tail Mountain. All the supplies were dropped by parachute. Two years later, I was a division boss on the Indian Creek Fire in Yellowstone Park. Bill Orr came as the other division boss. He brought with him a first-year ranger from Big Bend National Park, C.W. "Bill" Wendt, who had been a smokejumper for the Forest Service at Missoula. Wendt was later the chief ranger in Yosemite National Park. I consider him the best all-around ranger I have ever known.

In 1967, I had a 570-man fire camp on the Flathead Fire. Bill Wendt and Lee Shackleton, later the law enforcement officer in Yosemite, both worked out of this camp, as did Don Cross, later the Yosemite fire control officer. The following year, I was in northern Alaska helping the Bureau of Land Management contend with lightning-caused tundra fires in the Dall sheep and caribou range. Bettles Field, our base camp, is thirty-five miles north of the Arctic Circle. I was flown there in a twin-engine Cessna from Fairbanks, then out on the Jim River to the northeast by helicopter. Next they took me up on the Koyukuk River to fires thirty miles north of Bettles.

On these fires, and on the Flathead Fire, I had helicopters at my disposal. They would pick up and deliver men to fires and make emergency trips anywhere, as they could land anywhere. On the Flathead Fire, they were sent often to scare grizzly bears away from crews that were being threatened by them. I often thought what a change in transportation from what I had seen in my early years with the service. Up on the Koyukuk River, I did low-flying reconnaissance in helicopters. One weekend I spent thirty-two hours in them, often flying only twenty feet from the ground, many large Alaska moose beneath us.

In October 1969, I made the decision to retire from the National Park Service after thirty-seven years, with thirty-four of them at Glacier. Mel Ruder, the Pulitzer Prize–winning owner of the *Hungry Horse News* in Columbia Falls, who had accompanied me on many backcountry trips through the years, wrote in his news item about my retirement that I am "the man who best knows Glacier National Park's 1,000 miles of trails." Writing about my relationship with my trail crews and park visitors through the years, he kindly added that he had observed me to have a "strong loyalty to his men" and that "his courtesy to park visitors is unfailing."

DURING THE 1970s, I worked summers for Bud Ellman, Glacier's horse concessionaire, and in the fall hunting season for Bob and Donna Toelke, outfitters, as their main line packer, packing thirty miles into the Bob Marshall Wilderness from Holland Lake. I worked on summer pack trips for outfitters Bob and Kathy Smith, also in the Bob Marshall, and month-long stints during hunting season in the Bob for the Forest Service, working under Jack Dollan, the Wilderness ranger.

While working for Bud Ellman in Glacier, I covered many of the same trails that I had while working for the Park Service. I have took out many private multiple-day pack trips, including two with U.S. Senator Max Baucus. I got to know the senator well, and the two of us became close friends. I visited him at his office in Washington, D.C., in 1980 and again in 1985.

During the summer of 1979, a decade after his retirement from the National Park Service, W.J. Yenne spent several weeks guiding a team from the U.S. Geological Survey throughout Glacier National Park. He is seen here at the top of Boulder Pass with horse concessionaire Scott Ellman and geologist Omer Raup from the USGS Office of Energy Resources in Denver. *Omer Raup.*

I had some interesting experiences while I was guiding for the concessionaires. One time, when I was guiding out of Many Glacier, I had two new student guides with me, as well as a family from New York with three children. There had been a blonde grizzly seen near the head of Sherburne Lake, so I told them all to watch for it. As we were coming back from Cracker Lake, one of the little kids, the smallest of the bunch, said, "There's something over there."

As we looked, the grizzly stood up. There was an open, grassy slope nearby, so everybody got a good, long look before the bear dropped down on all fours and ambled away.

That night, the two student guides told everybody they saw around the Many Glacier Hotel how close we had been to that grizzly. When I came down to take care of some business at the transportation desk, people started asking me whether I had been afraid. I laughed and said, "Well, no, there were eight of us and I was riding the fastest horse."

Over at the Lake McDonald corrals, we had a two-year-old black bear that hung around. He was kind of tame, and we would see him along the trail. One day, when I was coming back to the corrals with a fairly large party, I heard the two teenage boys whom I had put at the end starting to laugh and chuckle. I looked back and saw that this harmless little black bear was following along not twenty feet behind their horses, which is something that he did once in a while. Of course, word spread up toward the front of the party, and someone exclaimed, "There's a bear following us."

It was a startling thing for people who had never seen a bear, but nothing happened. I've had my pack string scattered by a grizzly, but only because the bear ran up to them inadvertently and spooked them. I have never known of any bear attacking a person on a horse.

There is a story that was told about packing a huge sink up to Sperry Chalet. It was credited to me, but I only retold it a time or two. It was when I was working for Bud Ellman. Since this sink weighed about 400 pounds and was too big for a pack horse, he built a travois like the Plains Indians used to use when they moved camp and hitched it to a good-sized draft horse that was broke to the harness. He wrapped the sink in canvas and tied it to the travois. He was dragging it up the trail when he met some people hiking down. As the story goes, they started asking some questions, so Bud Ellman, feeling playful, told them about a Blackfeet chief who had died and wanted to be buried up at Sperry Glacier. These people later stopped at Park Headquarters and told the ranger on duty that this man deserved a lot of praise for going to all that trouble just for the last wishes of the chief.

The author leading a pack string in Montana's Bob Marshall Wilderness on July 19, 1987.

Around that time, I also had an amusing incident of people asking questions that demanded a wry response. On the trail up to Sperry Chalet, I had a four-year-old Appaloosa horse in my pack string. People familiar with Appaloosas know that more often than in other breeds, the sclera, the part of their eyes surrounding the iris, appears white when the eye is in a normal position. Horsemen call this "glass eyes." This little guy was a gentle horse, but he had never been in the mountains, so every time he saw a strange-looking tree or rock, he was ready to head back home. He'd be right alongside the front pack horse before I could get him stopped.

I had gotten up to the switchbacks below the chalet when I came around a curve and met a bunch of hikers with packs and different-colored clothes. They were in the trail and on both sides, and when this little Appaloosa saw them, he really headed for home. He went about two horse-lengths before I could get him stopped, and I finally got him straightened out.

It seems that in every large group of people, there is always one guy who knows it all, and he tells everybody what he knows. He started making fun of my horse, asking, "What kind of a horse you got there?"

Every question he'd ask, all the people would look at him and then at me. When I said that he was just a young horse who had never been in the mountains before, this man asked how old he was.

"Well, you can see that his eyes haven't turned brown yet," I replied, tongue in cheek. "*You* know how old a horse is when his eyes turn brown, don't you?"

Everyone looked at him for an answer. He had none.

IN THE FALL OF 1978, I was invited to be the guest of the Park Service in Yosemite National Park. The invitation came from Bill Orr and Bill Wendt, whom I had first met two decades earlier. Orr was now the regional head of Resource Management and Visitor Protection in the San Francisco office, and Bill Wendt was chief ranger at Yosemite. We spent five full days of the week in the Yosemite backcountry. Bill Wendt was the packer and proved to be a good stock hand. They used sawbuck saddles and the old one-man diamond. I'd had enough sawbuck experience that I made a pretty good helper. All the fellows on the trip were versatile and knew their jobs better than any park rangers I had seen since the 1940s.

The original invitation turned into VIP ranger contracts, and I accompanied Bill Wendt on his fall backcountry inspection and hunter patrol trips along the east and north boundaries of Yosemite nine times through 1988. In October 1979, near Sasche Spring, we caught two deer hunters who had come into Yosemite through the Stanislaus National Forest. In the early years, it was often just the two of us, but in 1988, there were twelve, including two packers who had a nine-mule pack string.

In the spring of 1984, I attended the Seventh Horse Mounted Patrol Training Course in Yosemite, a six-week course designed for field personnel that goes from basic to advanced horsemanship. It is aimed at the effective utilization of the horse in public relations, search and rescue, law enforcement activities and backcountry activities. As Bill Wendt explained to me, each year the course is "named after an individual who had made a contribution to the National Park Service in the field use of saddle and pack stock." In 1984, I had the honor of seeing them name it the "Bill Yenne Session." As he later told me in a letter, the attendees enjoyed my "good humor, companionship, and energy," adding that "the members of the class, with whom you roomed, appreciated your company and have said so."

I'm lucky to have the Park Service remember all the hard work I did for it through the years.

Former Glacier National Park superintendent Bob Haraden and W.J. Yenne on Apgar Mountain overlooking Lake McDonald in August 1988.

IN 1979, I PACKED and guided a U.S. Geological Survey party through the most remote sections of Glacier Park for three weeks. During the three weeks I was with the USGS party, at least half of our night camps were in grizzly country. At one of our sites, a man was killed and completely devoured by bears shortly after we'd been there.

Our most frightening incident occurred on our first day out. My pack mules were very heavily loaded, and we went from Lake McDonald to Gunsight Lake that first day. A short distance east of the Continental Divide at Gunsight Pass are some of the steepest and most dangerous snowfields in the Park. The trail crew, camped at Gunsight Lake and assigned to that beat, had made a tread across these dangerous drifts barely wide enough for a very agile person to cross safely on foot. I had no other choice than to cross, as there was no way I could turn back on that steep snow. At a place where the cliffs below were the steepest, my stock actually had to jump upward some three feet to stay on the narrow tread. I had instructed the riders coming behind the pack mules to stay on their horses. Most were

W.J. Yenne sharing a humorous story with U.S. Senator Max Baucus of Montana at the senator's Washington, D.C., office in the fall of 1985. The author took the senator on several backcountry horse trips in Glacier, and the two became close friends. After one such trip in 1979, Baucus wrote, "I don't know what I enjoyed more—the beauty of the park or your humor. I sometimes even wonder if you let that mare slip her halter just to keep things interesting." Therein lay a tale.

inexperienced in riding, and I feared for the risk in getting them dismounted in this dangerous situation.

Some of the trail crew told me later that they had been told by someone that a party was coming over on Tuesday. However, a week before that, we had had a five-hour meeting with Park Service and USGS personnel present, and everyone had been given a copy of our itinerary. Someone there had assured me that the trail would be ready on Sunday.

Toward the last part of our outing, I had a similar experience beside Paiota Falls on the Stoney Indian Pass Trail. We were camped at Mokowanis Junction, and I had taken some of the geologists up there and brought the empty horses back. The geologists were to hike back by a cross-country route. In that set of switchbacks, at the steepest part, a large chunk of sod, gravel and brush had slid down and blocked the trail. There was a small trail crew camped near us, at Upper Glenns Lake campground. I reported this to them and a young seasonal ranger who was with them. They did not seem interested, and the next morning when I again told them about

Yosemite National Park superintendent Bob Binnewies, W.J. Yenne and Yosemite chief ranger Bill Wendt in May 1984. The author was in Yosemite that month for the "Bill Yenne Session" of the National Park Service Horse Mounted Patrol Training Course.

it and was told that they did not plan to go up that way, I tried to borrow a mattock from them. I was told that they did not lend tools.

I had with me a large double-bitted axe and a small shovel, the kind used with Pulaski tools in firefighting. When we got up there to where the trail was blocked by the slide, Bob Earhart, head geologist, and I went to work with the axe and the small round point shovel clearing the slide material to allow us to cross. We spent at least two hours doing this. Needless to say, the double-bit axe was a wreck when we had finished. Later I told Bob Burns, Glacier's visitor protection (law enforcement) specialist, of this incident. He shook his head and laughed, not in surprise, but thinking of his college years at the University of Montana, in which he had worked summers on Glacier's trails, years in which we maintained all of the trails. Bob's crew was one of the very best, and to it was entrusted many of the most difficult assignments. He laughed to think of the changes that can take place over the years.

One person who had wished to join our pack trip into the Bob Marshall Wilderness in August 1982 with Bob and Kathy Smith was actress Jeanette Nolan McIntire. However, at that time, she and her actor husband, John McIntire, were going on location for six weeks in the making of the Clint

W.J. Yenne with Bob Toelke in the Flathead National Forest south of the Middle Fork of the Flathead River on July 28, 1987.

Eastwood movie *The Honky Tonk Man*. The McIntires have a summer place located in the Yaak country of northwestern Montana near the British Columbia border. I had the pleasure of being an invited guest at their house, and no finer hosts could one find.

Each December for many years I have gone to Oklahoma City to attend the National Finals Rodeo and the awards presentation to the new world champions in rodeo, as well as, at that time to attend the enshrinement ceremonies of the year's honoree or honorees into the National Cowboy Hall of Fame. I am very proud to be a charter member of a group that has become known as the "Rodeo Hall of Fame Wild Bunch," a charter that was founded at the Hall of Fame in 1966.

Jack Dollan, mentioned earlier as Wilderness ranger in the Bob Marshall Wilderness, transferred to the National Park Service a few years ago and is assigned to the Guadalupe Mountains area in Western Texas near Carlsbad Caverns. In the fall of 1982, he invited me to come to visit him there when I left Oklahoma City. I had an opportunity to ride some of the forty-seven miles of trails he had just completed in this newly established National Park Service area. I consider myself very fortunate to have the opportunity of continuing to explore more new trails.

I recall being at a mountain pass in Yosemite National Park between Tower and Forsyth Peaks with Chief Ranger Bill Wendt and Ron Mackie, senior backcountry ranger, and being asked how many trail miles I had logged in my lifetime.

I answered a question with a question by asking, "Do you mean counting today?"

Friends and family gathered for William J. Yenne's memorial at Triple Divide Pass on July 31, 1995. *Back row*: Gerald Yenne, his nephew; C.W. "Bill" Wendt, retired chief ranger, Yosemite National Park; Joseph L. "Bill" Orr, former chief ranger at Big Bend National Park and retired regional head of Resource Management for the National Park Service; and Art Burch Jr. of the Glacier Park Boat Company. *Front row*: William P. Yenne, the author's son; his granddaughter Annalisa Yenne; and Art Burch Sr., the owner of the Glacier Park Boat Company, with whom the author had worked during his retirement.